gaz regan's
Annual Manual
for Bartenders

2012

gaz regan's
Annual Manual for Bartenders
2012

gaz regan

mixellany limited

Copyright © 2012 Gary Regan

All rights reserved. Printed in the United Kingdom. No part of this book may be used or reproduced in any manner whatsoever without written permission except in the case of brief quotations embodied in critical articles and reviews. For information address Mixellany Limited, 3 Eyford Cottages, Upper Slaughter, Cheltenham, Gloucestershire GL54 2JL United Kingdom..

Mixellany books may be purchased for educational, business, or sales promotional use. For information, please write to Mixellany Limited, 3 Eyford Cottages, Upper Slaughter, Cheltenham, Gloucestershire GL54 2JL United Kingdom. or email jared@mixellany.com

First edition

ISBN 13: 978-1-907434-01-3

British Library Cataloguing in Publication Data.
A catalogue record for this book is available from the British Library.

This year's manual is dedicated my girlfriend, Amy. She who puts up with my bullshit and lets me be me.

Thanks, Babe. I'm so happy we found each other.

ACKNOWLEDGMENTS

Once again Martha Schueneman, my trusty editor, has to be highlighted here. We work together so damned well. Thanks Ms. M. Thanks once again also to Jared Brown and Anistatia Miller for being fabulous publishers, and good friends. And this year I get to thank Pilar Zeglin and Simon Webster, the sales team, one on each side of the Atlantic, who helped fund this project by selling ad-space within these pages. I'd be remiss not to also thank the fabulous companies who bought the ad-space, too. Your help is very much appreciated, guys. I hope that the bartenders who read this year's manual will continue to support your fine products.

By the Same Author

The Cocktailian Chronicles: Life with the Professor

The Book of Bourbon & Other Fine American Whiskies

gaz regan's Annual Manual for Bartenders, 2011

TABLE OF CONTENTS

Part 1
   A Serialized Autobiography:
   Some Adventures on New York's Upper East Side
   in the Seventies   15

   Chapter 3
      Time to Move to the Big Apple   17

   Chapter 4
      Drake's Drum Gets a New Bartender   25

   Chapter 5
      Tales of Various and Sundry
      New York Bartenders in the Seventies   35

   Chatper 6
      Tales of the Underworld,
      & a Certain David Brooks   49

Part 2
   The Mindful Bartender   57

   Chapter 1
      Mindful Bartending   59

   Chapter 2
      Bartender Quotes of the Year   79

   Chapter 3
      Bartenders' Bartenders of the Year   95

Chapter 4
Fabulous Bartender Awards   123

Chapter 5
Bar Blogs of the Year   219

Part 3
Bar Geekery   241

Chapter 1
Scuppered: A Tale of the Bar Rail   243

Chapter 2
On Giggers and Jiggers and the Fine Art of Free-Pouring   249

Chapter 3
Ingredient Focus: Japanese Whisky   263

Index   000

PART 1 • A SERIALIZED BIOGRAPHY

gaz regan's
Annual Manual for Bartenders
2012

INTRODUCTION

Well, I really painted myself into a corner by making this manual an annual project. Putting out a new book every twelve months is not an easy chore at all. Nevertheless, with the help of myriad folk it looks like we've managed to get this done in time to release it in May again this year, and we'll try to repeat this again in 2013.

Last year my picks for 101 Best New Cocktails was part of this book, but you won't find this year's recipes in this 2012 edition, I'm afraid. This year they are getting a book all of their own, and that book will hopefully be released in July.

As you're about to discover, I've gone all over the place in this year's *Annual Manual for Bartenders*, and I hope that you'll be happy to hear that my intention is to do the very same thing every year. I want this set of books to reflect what's going on each year within the global bartender community, and I've tried to highlight as many bartenders as possible, setting down what each and every one of them has brought to the table over the past year.

I've also set up a web page as a companion piece to this year's manual, and on it you'll find links to all sorts of extra information about various and sundry items that relate to the information you'll find within these pages. Go to http://

tinyurl.com/AM4Bartenders2012 and you'll see what I'm talking about.

Thanks to all you bartenders out there for your continuing support of the craft, thanks for pushing the envelope by introducing new products, new methodology, and new ideas that serve to teach us what our jobs are really all about.

Please try to always remember that when you choose to tend bar for a living, you choose to be of service to your guests, and that is the most important aspect of the craft. Everything else is secondary.

Part 1

A Serialized Autobiography: Some Adventures on New York's Upper East Side in the Seventies

In last year's **Annual Manual** I brought you through my first seventeen years on God's green earth, ending in 1968 when I dropped out of high school and my family moved to Thornton to take over the Bay Horse, the pub of my dad's dreams. If you didn't read that episode, before we go further you might want to know that my father's name was Bernard, my mother was Vi, and Nan, Vi's mother, lived with us, too. It was like having two mothers. I was a lucky lad.

Thornton is situated less than three miles from the Irish Sea on the northwest coast of England, and it's part of a township called Thornton-Cleveleys, a seaside resort. Our family had lived in Cleveleys until 1964, when I was twelve going on thirteen, and from there we'd moved about 50 miles inland to Bolton, an industrial town close to Manchester, where we took over The Prince Rupert, a pub full of character and characters.

Read on, then, and I'll take you through my next few years in England, and my first half-a-dozen or so years in New York Fuckin' City. What a blast I had there....

Chapter 3:

Time to Move to the Big Apple

A month or so after I decided to drop out of the educational system, I opted to jump back in by enrolling in a course at Courtfield, the culinary department of the technical school in Blackpool, which was just about ten miles from the Bay Horse. I was far more enamored of hanging out at the pub than I was with getting a decent education, so I dropped out of Courtfield after a couple of semesters and went to work for Bernard and Vi instead.

The Bay Horse had been a farmhouse once upon a time, and the building is three- or four-hundred years old, depending on who's telling the story. It's been renovated since we were there, but when we took it over in 1968, the Bay sported four rooms, each with its own personality, and it was a very authentic olde-worlde pub, complete with nicotine-stained beige walls, dark beams, horse brasses, and a row of pewter tankards that hung from the shelf above the main bar where we kept extra bottles of hooch, just in case. The clock behind the bar was set to being twenty minutes later than real time, and woe betide anyone who tried to correct that. "Everyone will miss their buses if you put that clock right," Beatrice, one of the barmaids, told me when I attempted it.

Vi and Bernard at the Bay Horse.

I helped out behind the bar when needed and I took care of the cellar at the Bay, but there wasn't enough work for me to say I actually had a job, so I invented one. I started serving meals at lunchtime and snacks in the evening, too. Prior to this, the only food available at the Bay was in the form of pork pies and Cornish pasties that were kept in a warming oven on the bar.

Luckily, I got a jumpstart on this business when a team of around twenty workers came to town to change every household's gas appliances so they would work with gas from the North Sea, rather than coal gas. Huge reserves of gas had been discovered under the North Sea in the early Sixties, and slowly but surely, everyone in the UK would be using it. When the work team descended on the pub looking for lunch, then, they put up with pies and pasties for one day after I promised them I'd have real meals for them if they came back the following day. I can't remember what I made, but it was probably something like Shepherd's Pie with vegetables. Whatever it was, it worked for them. They came back every day until they'd fitted out Thornton with the gas conversion kits.

By the time those guys left town, I'd also turned some locals onto my lunches, and since the pub wasn't too far from a huge compound of civil service offices and an ICI industrial factory, it didn't take long to build up a decent following. Bernard and Vi let me take over a small corner of one of their barrooms, and in short order, after borrowing money from the folks, of course, I installed a microwave—brand new upon the market in the late Sixties—a machine for making toasted sandwiches, an electric bain-marie for soups and stews, and a large warming oven to boot. I was my own boss, so it didn't feel as though I had a proper job, and the food station brought in enough scratch to buy all the beer I needed, so all was well with the world for the time being.

Then I fell in love. I met Norma Dransfield at a party, circa 1968, and on September 5, 1970, thirteen days before my 19th birthday, Norma and I were married. She had a keen sense of humor, a warm personality, and I think that she pretty much adored me. What could go wrong?

Bill Greenham, my best man, and me on my wedding day in 1970.

Three years later I ran away to New York.

Norma was a sweetheart, and during the almost three years we were married we opened a small restaurant together just down the road from the Bay Horse. It did fairly well once I got a liquor license that permitted my bar to stay open an hour later than the pub providing the punters ordered food, but I wasn't a hundred-percent happy. Something was nagging at me. What could possibly be wrong? I had a great wife, a small house, a thriving business, yet still I wasn't satisfied. I'd better give all this up and start over, I thought, so in the summer of 1973 I sold the restaurant, sold the house, left Norma, and went in search of Superman. New York City, here I come.

Dave Ridings, one of the Five Pints of Bitter Lads from the Prince Rupert, had emigrated to New York in '68, the same year we'd moved into the Bay Horse, and he and I had kept in touch all along. Whenever he came back to Bolton to see his family, he'd always pop over to Thornton and spend a few days at the pub. He'd gotten himself a job as a bartender in New York, working at a joint called Drake's Drum on Second Avenue between 84th and 85th Streets. He'd regale us with stories of bar life in the Big Apple and he made us cocktails, no less. We'd never had cocktails. Bear in mind that this went down at the height of the hippie movement and you might get some idea of how fabulous were his stories, and how I, a small-town kid when it came down to it, was just longing to get a taste of Dave's life.

Dave Ridings at Drake's Drum, circa 1973.

In November of 1972, Vi took Norma and me to New York for a week-long vacation. It was my present for my 21st birthday. We spent much of that week in Drake's Drum, though we did a fair amount of sight-seeing, hitting a Broadway show and going to the top of the Empire State Building, too. And Vi and I met Richard Nixon toward the end of that week. He'd just been re-elected in a major landslide of a victory over George McGovern, and although Nixon turned out to be not quite the man we all thought he was going to be, at that point in history he was akin to a rock star to most people in the USA. When his car pulled up right in front of us on Fifth Avenue, just across the street from Saks, and he got out to do a walk-about, we were mightily impressed. He walked right over to a guy by my side, shook his hand, he then turned and shook my hand, and within seconds he was surrounded by secret service agents who formed a human corridor for him to walk down, shaking hands with the seemingly hundreds of New Yorkers who swarmed to get close to him. Women were screaming in the same manner you'd have expected if he'd been Paul McCartney.

That trip might have helped me decide to pack up and leave home a little, I guess. I had just fallen in love with New York Fuckin' City, and the thought of living there, coupled with the thought of being single and living there, not to mention the thought of being single, having an accent, and being a bartender in New York, was pretty compelling to say the least.

Fact is, I'd known that I wanted to live in New York since I was about eight years old. America back then got everything first, and we poor souls in England had to wait a few years for it to travel across the Atlantic. I don't mean that in a literal sense, but it seemed as though the USA in general, and New York City specifically, was already living in the future. Americans seemed to have more money than we did, and their gadgets, toys, and cars were bigger and better than ours.

When I realized that I'd married far too young—others of my generation married young, too, but we were in the minority—and that I needed to get out of my marriage, I also understood that this was the perfect opportunity to get my ass over to the Big Apple where I'd find fun and adventures, American women, and bars that didn't close until the wee hours of the morning.

By the end of September, 1973, I was Ridings' roommate in a walk-up railroad apartment on East 81st Street. We each had to pay 85 bucks a month for the rent. Life was about to become so very sweet.

BARDSTOWN BARREL SELECTIONS

WHISKEY-FLAVORED WHISKEY.

Redemption Rye	Redemption High-Rye Bourbon	Temptation Straight Bourbon	Riverboat Rye
95% RYE	38.2% RYE	75% CORN	95% RYE
5% MALTED BARLEY	1.8% MALTED BARLEY	20% RYE	5% MALTED BARLEY
92 PROOF	60% CORN	5% MALTED BARLEY	80 PROOF
	92 PROOF	82 PROOF	

Chapter 4

Drake's Drum Gets a New Bartender

Drake's Drum had opened 1968. It was owned by Jim Duke, a Liverpool lad with a mop-top haircut and Beatles accent that could charm the worm out of a bottle of mescal, and Frank Casa, a New York preppie kind of a guy with a contemplative personality and a very strange sense of humor. For instance, Frank had a 45 (that's a single record, vinyl recording, for you whippersnappers) of a song called "In the Alps" by Lawrence Welk and The McGuire Sisters. It was made in the fifties, and it was pretty hokey. No, it was very hokey. Very hokey, indeed. Frank would put this record onto the jukebox at the Drum, but he didn't ever list it. He'd put it into a slot that was reserved for "Jumpin' Jack Flash" or another popular song of the day, and when some unsuspecting customer pushed the right buttons and the record played, Frank would just smile quietly to himself and go about his business.

Frank Casa and Jim Duke, circa 1973.

Jim, on the other hand, was pretty straightforward. He had a good sense of humor and he was a good businessman, too. He came from humble beginnings in Liverpool, he had a good head on his shoulders, graduated from university in the UK—something I'm betting not many of his neighbors did—and Jim was determined to make money. Although both he and Frank enjoyed, to some extent at least, the celebrity aspects of being bar owners, neither of them ever lost sight of the ball. Drake's Drum was a business, first, foremost, and always.

The Drum took its name from "Drake's Drum," a poem by Sir Henry Newbolt (1862-1938), and lest anyone forget that Sir Francis Drake was the seafaring scoundrel who saved Britain from the Spanish Armada, behind the bar hung a large wooden sign emblazoned with a verse from the poem:

> Drake he was a Devon man, an' ruled the Devon seas,
> (Capten, art tha' sleepin' there below?)
> Roving' tho' his death fell, he went wi' heart at ease,

> A' dreamin' arl the time o' Plymouth Hoe.
> Take my drum to England, hang et by the shore,
> Strike et when your powder's runnin' low;
> If the Dons sight Devon, I'll quit the port o' Heaven,
> An' drum them up the Channel as we drumm'd them long ago.

The Drum was decked out in good old-fashioned nautical style. There were ropes, bells, and model ships wherever you looked, sawdust on the floor, a long copper-topped bar, and clusters of tables suitable for dining purposes, each one bedecked with a red-and-white checkered tablecloth and a Heinz ketchup bottle that contained ketchup, but usually generic stuff. Heinz is so expensive, you know.

The place was dimly lit, the only natural light coming from a couple of rows of small nicotine-stained windows that looked out onto Second Avenue, if you stood on your tippy-toes, that is. The ceiling was filled with "flags of all nations" that were taken down once a year for cleaning. This task was performed around March 17th in order to avoid a repeat performance of the ceremonial burning of the Union Jack that took place on one fateful St. Patrick's Day when a bunch of revelers took things a little far.

The food at the Drum was a mish-mash of British, American, and any other cuisine that might just sell: The Sir Francis Drake Steak and Ale Special, The Embellished Burger (with salad and fries), Polynesian Pepper Steak and good old Veal or Eggplant Parmigiana. It was edible—and it was cheap.

From Wednesday through Sunday, the bar at the Drum was at least three-deep by nine o'clock. It was packed with lots of neighborhood characters and packs of rugby players, mostly hailing from the UK, Ireland, Australia, and New Zealand, but there was a decent-sized pack of American rugby-ites, too. These guys attracted rugby groupies who, if there were no rugby players to be had, were usually willing to settle for one of the locals, and if they were willing to hang out till the bar closed at four in the AM, one of the bartenders might take them home for a few hours of nasty behavior. But although plenty of one-night-stands started out at the Drum, the place was, above all, a friendly neighborhood pub. It had that indefinable atmosphere that can be attained only when the owners, barstaff, and servers all get along well, have fun while they work, and actually like and care about most of their customers.

Although I'd begun working behind the bar at the Prince Rupert when I was fourteen years old and I'd kept my hand in ever since, when I ran away to New York in 1973 at the ripe old age of 22, I didn't have a clue about how to make even the most basic of cocktails. Okay, I knew how to make a Champagne Cocktail with a sugar cube and some Angostura bitters—Vi always added a little cognac to the glass, too—and we made Pimm's Cups and Whisky Macs (scotch and green ginger wine served at room temperature), but apart from those drinks and a few highballs such as Gin & Tonic, served with one or two ice cubes but never more than that, I was a bartender who knew best how to pull pints of ale and how to deal with customers. Margaritas, Dry Gin Martinis, Manhattans, and the like were completely beyond my ken.

"Sit at the service end of the bar and watch," Dave Ridings told me. And that's exactly what I did. Since I was Ridings' new roommate and didn't yet have a job, the staff put me on "scholarship," so I drank for nigh-on nothing. My education consisted of spending night after night after night on a stool at the far end of the bar, right next to the spot where the servers ordered their drinks. From there I could hear which drinks they were ordering and I could watch the bartender make them. In this way, I learned how to make Whiskey Sours, Grasshoppers, Brandy Alexanders, Singapore Slings, Russians Black, and Russians White—Mudslides had not yet been invented since Bailey's Irish Cream wasn't around in 1973—and I learned how to shake and how to stir, which glasses were used for what drinks and which garnishes went where, and I learned how bartenders dealt with their customers in New York Fuckin' City. I was having a blast.

Bar at Drake's Drum.

The difference between American and British bartenders at that time, to a large degree, was that the man or woman behind the bar in the USA was in command of the ship. In the UK it used to be (and still is in many pubs) the boss who typically played this role. This was how my parents, particularly my father, had run his pubs, and in 1973 I had to learn the American way of tending bar in more ways than one. Mixing drinks wasn't the only thing that was new to me, and in some respects it certainly wasn't the most important thing I'd have to learn, either.

Dave Ridings was a quintessential New York bartender. He was very popular with the ladies but he was loved by the guys, too. He was a rugby player, a good drinker who seldom really went overboard, an actor who studied with Terry Schreiber—a man whose students later included the likes of Edward Norton, who once said that finding the Schreiber studio "proved to be an enormous blessing"—and although Ridings stood around five-eight in his stocking feet, he'd tell you he was five-ten and you'd believe him, even if you were standing right next to the man. Ridings was probably the most charismatic man I've ever known, and although it was he, to a large extent, who taught me much about tending bar New York-style, it was Kevin Noone, an Irishman of a certain ilk, who really put me through my paces.

After watching the service bartenders for a few weeks, I figured that I might be able to bluff my way through a shift or two. I asked Jim and Frank to consider me if and when there was an opening, and I was rewarded shortly thereafter with one shift a week: Saturday night early shift—from eight in the evening till one-ish in the morning. Kevin Noone joined me behind the stick at nine, and after taking a short break before I got off work, he stayed till the joint closed at three. In those days New York bars closed one hour earlier on Saturdays. It was due to some old blue law that was meant to ensure that people could get up in time to get their asses to church on Sunday, I think.

Kevin was a tough taskmaster behind the bar, and although he could be fun on the other side of the stick, anyone who worked with the man suffered the same treatment. Do it Noone's way or no way at all. I wasn't allowed to step foot over the invisible barrier that separated his territory—roughly two-thirds of the length of the bar—from mine. So, if I needed a Makeson stout, an item that was stocked only in Noone's section, I had to wait until he had time to get one for me. If I tried to sneak past him when he was too busy to help me, there was hell to pay. He would scream at me and tell me to "get the fuck back to your own end of the bar," basically humiliating me as much as possible. Noone also kept an eye on me when I was mixing drinks, and when I screwed up, he'd jump down my throat. I once served a Manhattan to a customer only to have Kevin reach over, grab the drink, and throw it, glass and all, into the garbage.

"You forgot to put bitters in there," he glowered.

The Manhattan wasn't the only drink I screwed up during my first few weeks at the Drum. I made Whiskey Sours with scotch, for instance, and nobody noticed until a cheeky redheaded waitress—Cheryl Geary, a woman I'm still in touch with in 2011—saw the bottle in my hand. In the UK, if you order a whisky, you'll always get scotch, so it seemed like a reasonable choice to me.

I also made a huge gaff early one Saturday evening, when Frank Casa ordered an Extra-Dry Martini, straight-up with a twist. This was unusual for Frank. He was never much of a drinker, and he usually waited until late at night before having, perhaps, a small cognac with a cup of coffee right before he went home. I never did find out whether he suddenly decided to have an early cocktail or if he was testing me to see if I could make such a complicated drink. If it was a test, I failed miserably.

I distinctly remember thinking that, since a Dry Martini was comprised of gin and dry vermouth, then an extra-dry version must call for extra—as in more—dry vermouth. The opposite, of course, is true. Extra-Dry, in barspeak, means extremely dry. Less vermouth. Always.

I made Frank's drink, using almost as much vermouth as gin and stirring it over ice for a good twenty or thirty seconds, thus making sure that the cocktail was well chilled and had attained enough dilution from the melted ice so that the drink was gulpable—the best way to drink a cocktails is "quickly, while it's still laughing at you," according to Harry Craddock, bartender at London's Savoy Hotel in the 1920s and 1930s—and I strained it into a well-chilled cocktail glass. Next came the lemon twist, which I dutifully twisted, yellow-side down, over the drink, releasing the essential oils from the zest and imparting a fresh lemon scent. I carefully ran the twist around the rim of the glass, and then floated it, yellow-side up, on top of the cocktail, which I served to Frank atop a clean white cocktail napkin. Frank took a sip.

"Could I see you at the end of the bar, please, Gary?"

At least he didn't embarrass me in front of the customers.

It wasn't long after I started working at the Drum that I had a yearning to get back home to see the folks. This was the first time I'd been away from my family for any length of time, and I missed being able to share my stories with them. My first bar shift was around the end of October, 1973, and when December rolled around I decided to go back to Limey-Land for Christmas. I didn't tell the family I was coming. I just showed up at the pub and walked upstairs to the flat where Vi, Bernard, and Nan still lived. I was rewarded by the best welcome a boy could ever hope for, and for about ten days I partied with the guys I'd been hanging with the previous summer, telling them wild tales of life in New York Fuckin' City, of the booze and the bars and the women and the booze and the bars . . . And I also spent time with the folks, eating, talking, and being a family the best way we knew how.

On Christmas day, after the obligatory huge meal of turkey, stuffing, roast potatoes, mashed potatoes, Brussels sprouts, carrots, gravy, and the like, we were waiting for Nan to bring out the Christmas pudding when Vi fixed me with her bright green eyes.

"Gary, you know that sovereign I have? The one on the gold chain?"

"Yes, Mum?"

"Well, if I gave that to you, would you wear it?"

I was very touched. This was a family heirloom. Before I could answer, though, Nan, who was just bringing us bowls of rich, fruity Christmas pudding with lots of custard sauce, chimed in.

"If you take that sovereign, Gary, you must never take it off. It belonged to your great-grandmother, did that sovereign."

"Okay, Nan. I'll never take it off. Promise." I'd known my great-grandmother fairly well, since she didn't die until I was about twelve years old, and although she lived a good fifty miles from us, she came to visit our family fairly regularly. She was a real character who would ask, "How do them little people get inside that television?" and other questions about things that baffled her about the twentieth century. I was quite moved, then, at the thought of having this little piece of history, and Vi promised to get it for me later that day.

Vi didn't get around to digging out the sovereign that day, and I'd forgotten about it until I was in the hallway of the flat above the pub about 24 hours later. My mother came out of the living room and told me to stay where I was while she got it for me. She disappeared into her bedroom, and returned a few seconds later, putting the sovereign into my hand.

Nan and Vi at the Bay Horse.

"Whatever you do, don't tell anyone that this belonged to your great-grandmother," she told me.

"Why not, Mum?" I asked.

"I lost that one last year when I was in Malta," she said, "I'd been to a party on a yacht, and I tripped on the gangplank as I was leaving. Ended up in the sea, and when they fished me out the sovereign had gone."

Vi and I giggled about this for a few seconds, then she told me the end of the story. "The sovereign I lost had Queen Victoria on it," she explained. "This one was minted in 1967. Queen Elizabeth the second. I've been trying to figure out how to get it out of the house before Nan takes a close look."

Vi fixed me with those eyes again, and we grinned large. I took the coin and I put it around my neck. It would be our little secret.

Chapter 5

Tales of Various & Sundry New York Bartenders in the Seventies

I'd gotten myself a day job as a messenger at the South African Consulate in New York before I went home for Christmas in seventy-three, and this meant that I had a diplomatic visa and I could leave the country and come back at will. When I returned to New York just after New Year, I hired myself a lawyer and she started filing the papers to get me a green card while I roamed the streets of Manhattan doing errands for the various and sundry South African diplomats. The job didn't pay well, but I was learning how to get around the city, bringing in enough money to pay the rent, and it was far better than having a desk job as far as I was concerned.

A typical day for me during these early months in New York started with working nine to five out of the consulate's midtown office, grabbing a bite to eat as soon as I got home, then falling asleep for a few hours in front of the television before heading out to Drake's Drum and various other Upper East Side haunts around eleven. I'd drink draft beer, Gin & Tonics, and the occasional glass of red wine while trying desperately to get laid, and if I wasn't successful I'd be home by four-ish to grab another couple of hours sleep before setting off to work at the consulate. There were a few occasions when I ended up at an after-hours joint—Kanpai, a cool place in the basement of a building on 84th between First and Second that was owned by a Japanese guy and an African American whose names I forget—and went to work drunk in the morning, but I managed to keep my job until I got my work papers, so all was well with the world.

My world was centered round the bars within a ten-block radius of Drake's Drum for my first few years in the Big Apple, and although the Drum was my home base, there were other joints on my radar that I'd visit pretty frequently. Brandy's ("Where Incredible Friendships Begin") is a gay bar these days, but that wasn't the case back then, and since it was just around the corner from the Drum and I knew all the staff there (which meant that the drinking was relatively cheap), that was one of the places where you'd often find me hanging out, listening to Jerome, an African-American singer/guitar player who performed there regularly, and exchanging banter with Warren the bartender, a Scottish waiter with a very dapper moustache named Jackie Roberts, and Vic, the guy who owned the place. I also hung at Pedro's, another joint that was no more than a stone's throw from the Drum, and this hole-in-the-wall was where we drank Tidal Waves—I don't know what was in them but they sure were strong—and the best fresh Banana Daiquirís in town, simply because they were made with bananas that had been left in the sun in the front window until they were thoroughly black and as sweet as honey.

The Mad Hatter, on Second between 77th and 78th, was another of my favorite watering holes during my first years in New York. The owners, Dan Sweeney and Tom Doody, were nice guys, but I went there to visit two of my very favorite bartenders, Norman Smyth, an Irishman who once tended bar naked for an hour with Dave Ridings at Drake's Drum on a bet ("I didn't get a date for months after that," he joked with me when I reminded him of this incident a few years ago), and Mickey Bayard, a charismatic guy with the biggest personality you ever did encounter. These guys eventually opened a joint of their own, but like me, they were far better bartenders than they were owners, so, sad to say, their business didn't last too very long.

I'd be remiss if I didn't pause here to tell the story about Mickey Bayard walking his malamute dog in Central Park circa 1972, since it's such a typical Bayard story and it deserves to be set down somewhere or other. I contacted Mickey while I was writing this just to make sure I had my facts straight, and it turned out that he was working on his own book of short stories at the same time. If you see Mickey's book, buy it—it's bound to be hilarious.

The story of Mickey's malamute goes like this: In the early 1970s, Mickey had let his dog off the leash somewhere in Central Park since there weren't many people around and the dog was usually pretty well behaved. It wasn't long before the malamute spotted a smartly dressed man buying a hot dog from a cart at the 72nd Street entrance to the park, and before Mickey knew what was happening the dog had leapt up and stolen this guy's snack right out of his hand. And since the ground was wet that day, the dog's paws were muddy, so after stealing the hot dog, there were muddy paw-prints on this guy's camel-hair coat.

Mickey Bayard with malamute.

Mickey grabbed the dog, pulling it away, and he grabbed a handful of napkins from the hot-dog vendor and proceeded to rub the mud into the guy's coat. The guy with the muddy coat, meanwhile, was being nice about the incident, and he told Mickey not to worry about it. "I have a couple of malamutes myself," he said. Mickey looked at the guy's face for the first time and he was pretty startled to see whose coat he was rubbing mud into. "You're Robert Redford!" he screamed (like a teenaged girl, Mickey says).

Since Mickey could charm the hind legs off of a donkey, and since Robert Redford, who was in town to shoot *Three Days of the Condor*, is, apparently, a very nice guy, the two of them strolled the streets together for a while, chatting about this and that. Their stroll took them past the very fashionable Finch College, and lots of girls were hanging out of the windows screaming to Robert Redford as he and Mickey walked past. Redford waved up at them, and at this point he and Mickey shook hands and started to head in different directions, but a few of the Finch girls, who were regulars at the Mad Hatter, started screaming for Mickey instead of Robert, and since most of the students from this college went into the Mad Hatter on a fairly regular basis, the screams for Mickey ended up drowning out the screams for Robert Redford. Redford turned and nodded to Mickey. Mickey smiled back. "You're in my town, now, Bob," he said.

It didn't take too very long for me to get a few more shifts at the Drum, thus allowing me to leave the consulate job and become a full-time bartender. My fellow bartenders over the next few years included Scott Lamb, a dapper little guy with a keen wit who once ordered twelve Screwdrivers to sip alongside his brunch at a neighborhood bar. When he was told that they couldn't serve him a dozen drinks at once, he asked how many they could serve him, and he settled for four. Over the course of that brunch he ordered two more rounds of drinks, of course. Scott took his own life sometime in the 1980s, and I've lost track of Don, his older brother and a larger-than-life character in his own right.

Billy Wolter was another guy who worked the stick at the Drum, and Billy was always up for fun and mischief at work, as well as when he was on the other side of the bar. He was one of those guys whose wheels were always turning—you could almost hear them—and whenever he saw the opportunity to crack wise, make a deal, or go off on an adventure, Billy would fearlessly follow his gut. A very interesting character was Billy Wolter. Billy and his wife Linda moved to San Francisco in the late Seventies, and although we didn't keep in touch on a regular basis, we did meet up from time to time. Billy died in February, 2011, and in his memory I penned a piece for the *San Francisco Chronicle* about my old friend:

San Francisco lost a truly great bartender in February when Billy Wolter, a man with whom I worked behind the bar in New York in the Seventies, succumbed to cancer.

Billy and I worked together at Drake's Drum, a fabulous Upper East Side neighborhood saloon, and on the street—he was raised in that part of town—he was known as the Mayor of Second Avenue. Billy was well loved in New York by everyone lucky enough to know the man.

For a few years back in the Seventies I teamed with Billy to throw Thanksgiving Day meals for any and all of our customers who had nowhere else to go. They were pretty riotous parties, too, catering to anywhere between twenty to forty hungry waifs and strays, each of whom would bring a little something to drink, of course. One year we had to roast two massive turkeys and a whole suckling pig in order to feed the masses.

When Billy and his wife, now widow, Linda Zanko, moved to San Francisco, his friends, myself included, were skeptical about him being happy outside of the Big Apple, but he was a man with a very magnetic personality, and it took him no time at all to find a job, and build a new network of friends who loved him.

I asked Linda to compile a list of bars where Billy Wolter worked during his thirty-plus years in San Francisco, and if you've ever been to any of the following joints you might have been lucky enough to meet him. If so, I'm betting that you remember him well. Bill worked at Morty's, Perry's, Liverpool Lil's, The Brazen Head, Reno Barsocchini's, Mulhern & Schachern, The Washington Square Bar & Grill, Point Reyes Roadhouse, The Lark Creek Inn, and Brix. Quite a line-up, huh?

Billy was typical of bartenders of my generation—we weren't cocktailian whizzes, but we knew how to show our guests a good time. Nevertheless, my old pal did win a drinks competition over twenty years ago. Something that I certainly never accomplished.

I last saw Billy about three years ago when he and I met for a good old catch-up chin-wag at Perry's, and he told me about winning a trip to Ireland for creating the Nutty Irishman, a drink made with Bailey's Irish Cream and Frangelico hazelnut liqueur. The drink can be made as an on-the-rocks cocktail, it can be topped with whipped cream, and it can also be served as an Irish-Coffee-style drink. I prefer the latter, personally, and I add a decent shot of Irish whiskey to it, too.

When I asked Linda about the Nutty Irishman, she confirmed that Billy had won a trip to Ireland with the recipe, but he'd collaborated with Cyril Boyce, his fellow bartender at Perry's, to come up with the formula. The two of them had a whale of a time in Ireland, apparently.

So long, Billy. It was a privilege to have known you, my friend. Save a barstool for me at that great stretch of mahogany in the sky. It's my round, I think.

My fave waitresses at the Drum included the aforementioned Cheryl "Big Red" Geary, Marie-Claire Nivelle, Sally Flynn, a wonderfully crazy Australian dancer by the name of Trish Jones, and Claudia Campbell Fucking Craig. Claudia, a very smart woman who is now one of the world's leading experts on the subject of fibromyalgia, and has authored and co-authored books on the subject—Google "Claudia Marek"—was well known back then for being loud and somewhat crazy, but people who took time to banish a bat or two from Claudia's attic found an extremely thoughtful intellectual lurking within. Her loud side, though, could prove to be very entertaining at times.

Trish Jones, the dancer.

Claudia was waiting tables at the Drum one afternoon and Ridings was on duty behind the stick. The Drum wasn't busy, and Dave was on the phone talking to the bartender at Dorrian's Red Hand, a bar just across the street from the Drum, while Claudia was screaming for him to make some drinks for one of her tables. Ridings ignored Claudia, repeated her order to the bartender on the other end of the phone, and continued to talk on the phone while his bartender buddy fixed Claudia's drinks and got a waiter to carry them over to the Drum on a tray.

"Here you go, Claudia," said the waiter as he put the drinks down in front of her at the service bar. "Could you keep your voice down just a little, please?"

The incident that probably best displays Trish Jones' wonderful brand of insanity took place on a hot summer's day when the sky turned a dramatic shade of dark green and rain fell in waves, rather than torrents. A group of seven or eight people took shelter from the storm under the awning that led to the front door of the Drum, and Trish took it upon herself to take a tray full of lighted candles to them. After distributing the candles among these somewhat bewildered people, Trish then made them all join her in singing Christmas carols.

But it was Dave Ridings who loomed largest in my life during the Seventies. I'd known him since I was about fourteen years old—he was about five years older than I—and he was the guy who had treated me as an adult when it came to exchanging ideas and having serious conversations, while at the same time he'd trick and tease me, embarrass me in front of a crowd, and make me groan when, for instance, he read one of my stupid poems out loud to a bunch of friends. As a teacher, and Dave Ridings was most definitely one of my teachers, he was the sort of guy who would never answer questions directly, opting instead to lead you down a path that might show you a way in which you'll find the answer for yourself. In all honestly

I didn't realize how big of an influence Dave Ridings had on me until years after his death in 2000. And I'm still trying to figure out his true role in my life. I speak to him regularly when I meditate. He still teases me.

Although Kevin Noone taught me about bartending and earned my respect through fear, Ridings taught by example, and he earned my respect through his extraordinarily compelling character. It was he who stressed over and over and in thousands of different ways that the job of a bartender was not to serve drinks, it was to serve guests. Ridings was the guy who looked after each and every one of his customers, offering advice when needed, getting one customer to walk another customer home if that was called for, and keeping a close eye on the grifters and the petty thieves who would pop into the Drum from time to time.

The grifters were many, and their schemes were obvious most of the time. A guy would wave a twenty in the air to get your attention, but when he actually paid for his drink, he'd pay with a ten. The bartender would make change on the ten, and the con-man would protest, hoping that the guy behind the stick would remember seeing a twenty in his hand, and just fork over the extra sawbuck. Ridings' method of dealing with this con, if the guy insisted he was right—sometimes they'd back down if you called them on it—was to tell the grifter that he was going to count out his whole register, take a reading, and if he was ten bucks heavy, he'd hand it over. At this point people around would start groaning because everyone knew that they wouldn't be able to get a drink for the next ten or fifteen minutes, and usually the grifter would say something like, "That's okay, I'll come back tomorrow and if you're over at the end of your shift, you can give it to me then." And although that would be the last time that particular crook would show his face at the Drum, you could bet your bottom dollar that the same scene would be played out again with another wise guy within a week or two.

My favorite scam to witness went down a few times a year at the Drum back then. A guy would sit at the bar and he'd produce an "envelope full of foreign coins that I just found on the street. They're all in jackets with prices on them, but I can't be bothered to go to a coin dealer, wanna give me twenty bucks for the lot?" The envelope would contain a bunch of coins, all in small cardboard jackets, and each one would be marked with a price so that it looked as though there was a couple of hundred dollars' worth of coins in there, but of course they were all worthless. Ridings would get rid of these guys in short order, usually by telling them that he'd seen them doing the same thing in another bar.

One regular thief would ask for a menu and stand at the bar perusing the bill of fare, and using it as a shield of sorts as he stole money from the bar. We never actually caught him in action, but after he'd been in a few times, always leaving without buying anything and with money missing from the bar every single time, we knew what was going down. The next time he came in, Ridings gave him a menu, then just stood there staring at him. People were shouting for drinks but he simply ignored everyone else at the bar and stared at the suspected thief. The guy soon figured out what was going on and he left pretty quickly. We never saw him again.

If one of these artful dodgers stole any money from the bar, Ridings considered it his responsibility, and he'd replace it from his tip-cup. Ridings, to a large extent, took over where Vi and Bernard had left off, teaching me by example about the importance of caring for your customers.

In 1974, Ridings decided to go on a trip around the world, and he teamed up with Tom McPartland, a fellow Brit, fellow bartender, and fellow prankster extraordinaire, to map out a route that would take them from England to Australia, mainly by road. The trip, which started in June of that year and took about seven months, gave Dave the chance to run the bulls at Pamplona, Spain, on July 7th, his birthday. He and Tom also traveled through Yugoslavia, Greece, Turkey, Iran, Afghanistan, India, Nepal, and Thailand, before arriving in Australia in December. At one border, though I forget which one, Ridings and Tom had a hunk of hashish that they'd bought from a local and they were spooked about getting through customs with it. One of them came up with a pretty nifty solution: They cut it into small-ish chunks, wet them down, and shook them up in a large bag of dehydrated beef stew they were carrying. Nobody would be able to tell the hash from the beef. The ploy worked, but from that point on, whenever they wanted to get high, they were never sure whether they were firing up hashish or dried beef.

Right before Ridings left for England to begin his grand tour, I took him out for a slap-up farewell dinner at Trader Vic's, then located in the Plaza Hotel on Central Park South. We drank tiki drinks, ate up a storm, and after dinner we headed for the Upper East Side, where we proceeded to drink ourselves silly in various neighborhood joints, ending up, of course, at Drake's Drum at around three in the morning. Ridings got lucky. Nicky Roe, a woman who would become his wife a few years later, was at the bar, and he ended up going home with her. I was not so lucky, and I ended up in The Cadillac, a coffee shop on York Avenue, for a drunken breakfast on my own.

I paid for breakfast with a ten-dollar bill that was so old it looked like it was about to drop to pieces, but the cheerful Greek guy behind the counter took it and handed me my change. I dropped him a decent tip and left to walk back to my apartment on 81st Street between York and East End. About a block before 81st I "felt" someone following me, and I turned around to see a guy, probably in his early thirties and fairly well dressed, walking behind me. I just knew he was following me, and I thought I was about to get mugged, but that was not the case. As I opened the ground-floor door to the apartment building I heard these words, "Stop, put your hands above your head, and turn around slowly. I'm a police officer."

Thus it was that I came to be arrested by a drunken off-duty transit cop who had been sitting next to me at the counter of the coffee shop. I was charged with passing counterfeit money. I spent the rest of the night and most of the following morning in the Tombs, and strangely enough I was the only guy in the cell in a three-piece suit. I was the only guy with an English accent, too. I think that my cell-mates—and there were at least a dozen of us in that cage—thought that I was a hit-man from out-of-town or something, since I was treated very well indeed by everyone there. Truth be told, though, everyone in that cell treated everyone else with respect. There was a sort of we're-all-in-this-shit-together camaraderie about the whole thing.

Dave Greenfield was, and I believe still is, a criminal attorney, and Dave Greenfield was a regular at the Drum. He was a great guy with a fabulous sense of humor, and his courtroom stories kept everyone entertained on a very regular basis. Dave was my one phone call after I was arrested, and he came down to the nineteenth precinct to be at my side as I was being processed. Dave assured me that the charge would not stick, even if the bill turned out to be phony, simply because I had another hundred-plus bucks in my pocket and none of those bills looked suspicious in the least. All I had to do was make it through the night.

My arresting officer, whose name I forget, kept passing the cell I was in, and as time went on, he began to sober up. And as he began to sober up, he started to feel sorry for me. He realized that the arrest was a bit of a screw-up. At one point he got me out of the cell to go get mug shots taken, and he took me to a tiny room down a hallway where a police photographer first told me to look directly at the camera, and then he instructed me to turn sideways while he took a profile picture. When I turned for the profile picture I saw a paper cup pinned to the wall with a notice pinned to it that declared that "gratuities for the boys will be gratefully accepted." I reached into my pocket and put a quarter into the cup.

"What are you doing?" asked the photographer.

"Tipping you. Thanks very much."

"You can't do that!"

"I tip everywhere I go in New York."

"No. You just can't do it."

"Does it constitute a bribe?"

By this time the photographer and my arresting officer were wearing big grins. I guess not many guests at the Tombs like to tease the cops.

When I finally hit the courtroom the next morning, Dave Greenfield was waiting for me, and he negotiated with my arresting officer before my case was called. It took him about two minutes. The case was immediately dismissed at the request of my new cop friend.

Chapter 6

Tales of the Underworld, & a Certain David Brooks

There were quite a few small-time hoods and bookies who hung around the bars I frequented back then, and most of them were nice enough and not too pushy. A small roundish guy with a boxer's nose who went by the name of Red once asked me to take bets on football games for him, and after I turned him down, "with all due respect, Red," he just smiled, told me that was fine, left me a decent tip, and the subject never came up again.

I did join in the football pool at Drake's Drum, though. Everyone who took part paid five bucks a week, we all had to pick the winner of every game played taking the point-spread into consideration, and the winner took the lion's share of the pot, with a few bucks going to whoever got the least number of games right. I didn't want to be a part of this pool, since I know nothing whatsoever about football, or any other sport on the face of the earth. I was cajoled into joining in when it first got started, just because the bartender who started it was a friend of mine and he needed to get as many people as possible to join in so that the pot would be decent. I won the first week. Everyone laughed. I won the second week. Everyone looked sideways at me. I won the third week. Now they were getting pissed. What could I do, though? I was picking teams by saying, for instance, that I thought that ravens could probably beat cardinals, or lions would make a meal out of panthers. My winning streak ended after that third week, but I ended up having a really good season overall. Ignorance is sometimes rewarded very well indeed.

The bookie-cum-hood who stood out from the rest of the small-time crooks crowd at Drake's Drum was a guy I'll call Harry. He was small, sharp-featured, nattily dressed, and carried an "equalizer," and although he had a couple of guys running numbers for him at the bar, Harry was into bigger stuff as well. I'm not quite sure what the bigger stuff was comprised of, and although he was low-level he was a real gangster, not just a bookie. Harry could be pretty scary when he wanted to be scary. People who rubbed him the wrong way got stares that would make most people's spine shiver.

One night when I was behind the bar, Harry and a bunch of his friends, including one of his runners, were having a few drinks, when I noticed Harry's body language change. I saw the dark look come over his face. I knew that all was not well. Next thing I knew Harry and one of his runners had left the bar, and one of the crowd told me that the runner wanted to quit his beat and that Harry had taken him outside to have a word. Next thing we knew, someone came racing into the bar to tell us that the runner was lying on the pavement in a pool of blood, around the corner, close to Brandy's. Harry never came back that night. The runner died from a gunshot wound.

That night turned into something of a nightmare for me and a bunch of others for the next few months. We were questioned by the DA on numerous occasions, and the defense lawyers for Harry came around to talk to us as well. They were scary characters who almost whispered their questions with deep throaty voices. I had to testify in front of a grand jury, and I had to testify again at Harry's trial. Since nobody ever came forward to say that they saw the shooting take place, all the evidence was circumstantial, and my two-cents' worth went nowhere at all. Harry had left way more money on the bar that night than he usually tipped, and the prosecution said that that went towards proving that he intended to come back to the bar, but never did, inferring that he ran after shooting his runner. The prosecution might have been right in their assumptions, but Harry was found not guilty when all was said and done.

I never saw Harry after the trial, thank God. And it was less than a year later that I was told that he'd been killed in a shooting incident. Two bullets. One in each eye. Harry had seen too much, I was told.

Not all of the crazy bastards who hung out at the Drum had a criminal bent. Some of them were rugby players. If you've ever hung at a bar where rugby players hang, you'll know that they can get very wild at times, and of all the rugby players who hung out at Drake's Drum in the mid-Seventies, none was quite as wild and crazy as David Brooks. Brooksie. When he returned to his native Australia, circa 1977, I told him he'd be missed, but he didn't believe me. "You'll forget all about Brooksie by next year," he said. Thirty years later I'm still telling tales about the lad. He was quite a character, was Brooksie.

Brooksie had spent some time in Bermuda, and he loved to tell us about the night when he and some of his friends broke into the rugby club there to steal some beer—all the bars had closed and the group was intent on partying into the wee hours of the morning. They broke a window, climbed into the clubhouse, grabbed a case of beer, and took it back outside where they sat on the grass and proceeded to drink the beer. Unbeknownst to them, they had tripped a silent alarm, and it wasn't long before a squad car came screaming through the night.

One of Brooksie's friends that night was a certain Viv Schindler. I've no idea how this guy spelled his name, and I never met the man, but for some reason I've always remembered that Viv Schindler was the name of the guy who tried to save the day that night. Viv Schindler, you see, was a big-time lawyer on Bermuda, and he couldn't afford to get arrested for stealing a case of ale. As soon as the cop car came to a halt, then, Schindler dashed over to chat with the police, and after explaining that the damage and the beer would be paid for first thing in the morning, the cops, who knew Schindler very well, agreed to not actually arrest anyone. "We have to take everyone's name and address, though," they told him. "But if everyone gives us a false name and address, well, we won't be able to find them, will we?" Schindler scurried back to his buddies, told them the scam, and the officer followed, complete with notebook, and started writing down everyone's name and address. Remember, this would have gone down in the early 1970s, so pen and paper would have been the norm for Bermudan police-people.

"George Smith, 22 South Shore Road," said the first guy.

"Jimmy Jones, 37 Chancery Lane," said the next.

On so on and so forth down the line. The last guy was Brooksie.

"Name and address?" asked the officer.

"Viv Schindler," said Brooksie, and proceeded to give the cop Schindler's actual address. Brooksie never took the story any further, but I'm pretty sure that Schindler never got into any real trouble.

Brooksie was always flirting with trouble, though, and he devised a fabulous bit of mischief that he used to pull in the men's room. If you're a woman you might not know this, but when men stand next to each other at a urinal, they make sure to look upwards so that nobody in the room could ever think that they are trying to get a glimpse of someone else's penis. God forbid we ever see another man's penis. Brooksie, though, all five-foot-seven of him, would make a point of staring directly at the penis of whoever stood next to him—providing he knew the guy, that is—and he'd always make a remark such as, "My God, Jim, how did you get that monster past customs?" So secure was Brooksie in his manhood that he didn't give a damn what anyone thought. And looking at penises in the men's room wasn't the only thing he did that would make most men uncomfortable. He also wore women's underpants—usually white cotton bikini briefs. He said they were more comfortable. People teased him about this, but Brooksie didn't care. He was a tough, hard-drinking, womanizing, Australian rugby player who didn't give a rat's ass about anything that was said about him. He might have been lacking in the height department, but he made up for that in the shoulders. He was cleancut, and I guess you might say he was ruggedly handsome, but I've never been good at being able to spot that sort of thing about other men.

Brooksie's panties came into view one night when I was behind the bar at Drake's Drum on a dreary Tuesday night in February, 1974. By two of the clock in the AM, the only customers left at the bar were a couple of waitresses who'd gotten off work at around midnight and were busy throwing back Screwdrivers, two local bartenders, one from The Mad Hatter, the other from Brandy's, and a half-a-dozen rugby players, Brooksie included. Everyone at the bar was pretty loaded. And Brooksie was out of commission—he had a broken leg. Nonetheless, he was regaling his fellow rugby-ites with tale after tale, and a pretty good time was being had by one and all at the bar. I'd had a couple of drinks myself and I was lapping up the scene. The Drum had an atmosphere I've seldom seen anywhere else. It was happy and friendly and it wasn't stupid. You'd hear conversations that ranged from Proust to Parisian whores in Drake's Drum, and they'd be intelligent conversations, too.

I was chatting with the two bartenders when a whoop emanating from the rugby players caused me to look down the bar to see what was going down. Brooksie, supported by crutches, was walking out of the men's room wearing only his plaster cast and his women's underpants. Nylon, these were. Not frilly, but see-through. White.

Everyone at the bar was laughing at Brooksie, who, should you need more visuals, was a very hairy bastard. He was a sight for sore eyes, that's for sure. Two of his rugby player friends went over to him and took him by the arms. They threw his crutches to the floor, carried him outside, took him to the other side of Second Avenue, and they left him there. Remember that this went down in February. It was freezing outside. And Brooksie had to hop back across the avenue to get back to the Drum. It took him a few minutes. Traffic had to stop for him, and this made his ordeal even funnier since the headlights of the cars became spotlights for the show. When he finally made it back into the bar everyone was screaming with laughter and applauding him for making it back.

Brooksie hopped onto a barstool, looked me in the eye, and cool as a cucumber, he said, "Gary, let me buy the boys a drink, would you?" Brooksie was a real class act.

Afterword

We'll leave it there for this year, then, though I've more stories of Drake's Drum and a few more Upper East Side bars to bring you next time around. When I look back on those days, I'm reminded of the camaraderie that existed between the staff and the customers at those neighborhood watering holes, and it makes my little heart glad. But before I close these chapters, I need to jump forward to the year 2000. I need to tell you about Dave Riding's wake.

Dave died of melanoma that year. He was living in the Midwest with Tina, his third wife. He had three sons by Sue, his second wife: Gareth, Owen, and Morgan. Kids he was very proud of, and rightfully so. I'm in touch with them today, though not very regularly, I'm afraid.

I decided not to go to Dave's funeral, and instead I organized a wake for him. It went down at Rathbone's, one of the joints we used to frequent back in the day, and a place that had retained its earthy neighborhood atmosphere for about thirty years at the time.

I spent about a month trying to get in touch with anyone and everyone who had known Ridings in the Seventies. There was no Facebook, and although e-mail was pretty common back then, not everyone had it. I spent many hours on the phone trying to track folks down, but it was the Internet that led me to most of the 100+ people who came to the wake. That's right, more than a hundred people, most of whom had not seen Dave Ridings since the late 1970s, came to the man's wake.

People flew in from England and Ireland, as well as Florida, California, Texas, and a few other states, too. People who hadn't seen each other for around twenty years came to town to honor David Ridings, a bartender who stood out among the crowd. A bartender who cared about his guests more than anything else. Ridings made pretty good Margaritas, but that's not what anyone remembered about him, or why they showed up that day. They remembered him as a friend, someone who was always there for them. Always.

Here in the second decade of the twenty-first century I'm happy to report that I still see lots of bars where the staff genuinely care about their guests. There's just as much fun going down in bars today as there was when I was in my twenties, and there are lots of bartenders who, like Ridings, will be remembered when they die for way more than the quality of their drinks.

Are you one of them?

Part 2

The Mindful Bartender

If you read the Mindful Bartending section in last year's **Annual Manual**, please excuse me for repeating myself a little here. I think it's important to give a brief outline of the concept of mindfulness for people who don't know what it's about, and for those who are familiar with it, if you're anything like me you might find that it's good to re-visit this philosophical stuff once in a while as a refresher.

This first chapter in the mindfulness section centers on my take on the subject, and it will be followed by quotes from other bartenders who display mindfulness in so many different ways, and a shout-out to this year's Fabulous Bartenders who have shown a great understanding of what their jobs are all about.

I FORGOT TO GET DRESSED

"I had one client, an English girl, who had a dressing gown that looked just like a street dress. She would sit at the bar, and after a few drinks would pull it wide open, leaving herself stark naked underneath. 'Oh, Jimmie,' she would say, 'I am so careless. I forgot to get dressed.' I cannot count the times I have had to wrap that dress around her and tie it securely. Your see it isn't easy, being a bartender."

—*This Must be the Place: Memoirs of Jimmie the Barman*, by Morrill Cody, 1937.

Chapter 1

Mindful Bartending

Mindfulness is a Buddhist concept that involves, more than anything, being totally aware of everything that's going on around you at any given moment. Many bartenders practice mindfulness without being aware of it—they are naturally mindful people, so it just comes naturally to them. These are the men and women who know intuitively what's going on with every single customer at their bar, and they're also aware of what the barback is doing, which guests are potential troublemakers, and who just walked into the bar. We've all seen this kind of bartender in action and they are a joy to behold. For the rest of us, mindfulness is something that must be learned, but worry not—it's fairly easy. Mindful Bartending can enhance our performances and rewards, without getting bogged down in deep philosophical jargon or concepts, so don't be afraid to embrace this concept.

When I wrote about this concept for the 2011 edition of the *Annual Manual*, I broke it down into the following categories: Mindful Connections, Mindful Mixology, and Mindful Fulfillment.

Mindful Connections

Mindfulness, as I apply it to bartending, encompasses connecting to yourself and others. I highly recommend spending time in meditation before setting foot behind the bar as a way to connect to yourself. Meditation can be sitting quietly, but it can also include setting up your bar, listening to loud music, or any number of ways in which you psych yourself up for the shift ahead. During your meditation, it's good to set your intentions for your upcoming shift. Concentrating on being of service to your guests is a good thing, for instance.

Another aspect of connecting with yourself is trusting your intuition. Listening is very important to Mindful Bartending, and when you listen to yourself, you're trusting your intuition. Ever serve a guest who you knew you shouldn't serve? Me, too. Intuition can't be measured, but we all know that it's a sense that we can usually trust. And the more you trust your intuition, the more your intuition will lead you in the right direction. Intuition is very important to the Mindful Bartender.

Communication is how we connect to others, and it is also key when practicing Mindful Bartending. I've found that two important aspects of Mindful Communication involve looking people in the eye when I speak to them and trying to spend as much time listening as I do talking, and you may find these actions enhance your life, too. Asking someone how they are doing and then walking away before they have a chance to answer is not part of the mindful practice.

And to continue on the connection front, it's good to practice Mindful Communication with absolutely everyone. Pop into the kitchen before your shift begins and say hello to the chef, the line cooks, and the dishwasher. Look them in the eyes and ask them how they are feeling. Listen to their answers, too.

Do the same with the servers and the barbacks and the checkout person at the supermarket and the homeless guy in the subway station. This sort of thing pays off big time.

Sticks and stones may break your bones, but words can break your heart. Try to remember this when you communicate with your guests, and try to be careful about how you phrase things. The word "should" is a good word to avoid, since nobody like to be told how they should behave. And you don't actually have to use the word "should"—implying it by telling someone flat out to, "Stop bothering those people," for instance, is also something that's good to avoid. The phrase, "you might want to think about" comes in handy when you're tempted to tell someone what you think they should do. "I wonder if you could think about lowering your voice a little," usually works far better than, "Hey, you should learn how to behave in public, asshole," for example.

Mindful Mixology

Mixing drinks mindfully might seem a little complicated initially, but it's actually quite simple, and it's something that I've seen many bartenders take to very quickly. Basically, Mindful Mixology is based on trusting your intuition when you are mixing drinks.

This concept can't work if you don't know what each ingredient you're working with tastes like, but if you have a good taste memory, and you're familiar with all of the ingredients in a specific drink, you can very likely bring them together in harmony by merely intuiting the ratios even if you've never made it before.

If you'd like to experiment with this concept, find a recipe for a drink you've never made before, and, disregarding the measurements in the formula, simply taste each of the ingredients then immediately make a cocktail with them. If you trust your intuition, there's a good chance you'll end up with a well-balanced cocktail, even if you use different proportions from the original recipe.

Mindful Fulfillment

Mindful Fulfillment is fairly simple, and it's key to keeping customers happy. Try to pay close attention to the individual tastes and preferences of all of your guests, and if you want to impress them by turning them on to a new drink, make sure that it's the sort of drink they'll appreciate. Trying to turn staunch Dry Gin Martini drinkers into Tiki fanatics, for instance, is something that can be achieved, but it's a task that needs to be accomplished very slowly, and in stages. I'd start by introducing them to a very dry Aviation, for instance, and work my way up from there. Thinking that such a drinker will really appreciate a Mai Tai straight off is probably not going to pay off.

In Conclusion

I'll end this short introduction to Mindful Bartending by reminding you that anger and happiness are both choices we make. If someone says something that angers you, it's good to remember that you have a choice as to how you react to every situation. Try counting to ten while silently thanking that person for giving you the opportunity to practice forgiveness.

If you choose happiness over anger, guess what will happen? That's right, you'll be happier. It's a pretty decent reward, I think.

Moving Forward

I've had one heck of a year trying to teach Mindful Bartending to anyone who will listen and simultaneously listening to bartenders from all over the world who have brought this practice into their craft. And I'm happy to report that the presentations, held under The Institute for Mindful Bartending banner—an entity formed last year by myself, Dushan Zaric, and Aisha Sharpe—have been very well received.

In the last twelve months I've held mindful talks—sometimes with Dushan and Aisha, sometimes without—in Dubai, Beirut, New York, Los Angeles, Chicago, and New Orleans. I'm writing this in November, 2011, and I'm expecting to go to Moscow next month to hold one last session of the year.

I think that one of the best moments I experienced in 2011 was in Beirut. I went down to the bar at my hotel to encounter two very excited bartenders behind the stick who couldn't wait to tell me that, after listening to my mindful workshop that afternoon, they had both meditated before coming to work. That kind of reward is priceless, indeed.

Seriously Speaking

I've been listening to some Ram Dass (see box below) audio books recently, and he has reminded me that it's a good idea to never take anything, myself included, too seriously. Mindfulness, for instance, is a serious endeavor, but if I can't laugh at myself for trying painstakingly hard to be mindful all the time, then I'm perhaps missing out on a lot.

Similarly, it's good to take our craft seriously, as long as we can also have fun, share some humor, and perhaps be inappropriate from time to time, just as long as we're pretty sure that no one will really take offence.

> Ram Dass is an American spiritual leader, and he's the author of several books, including the 1971 best-seller Be Here Now. Originally known as Richard Alpert, Ram Dass was a professor at Harvard who was dismissed after he and Timothy Leary, also a Harvard professor and also dismissed, actively promoted the use of hallucinogenics to students there.
>
> Ram Dass travelled to India, where he studied under Hindu guru Neem Karoli Baba, or "Maharaj-ji," and this was the man who gave Alpert the name Ram Dass, meaning "servant of God."
>
> Ram Dass suffered a stroke in the late 1990s, but he still teaches via his web site (RamDass.org), and at retreats in Hawaii, the state he now calls home.

Anger & Forgiveness

Ram Dass also taught me lots about anger and forgiveness recently, and this is something that I had, and still have, a hard time coming to terms with, but if I don't learn how to cope with anger, and how to truly forgive others, then I am hurting myself, and I'm not walking the path of the Mindful Bartender.

I was listening to *Experiments in Truth*—an audio book that's comprised of eight significant lectures that Ram Dass gave before his stroke in the late 1990s—and during one of these presentations he talked about having a particular hatred for a certain politician.

In order to rid himself of this hatred, Ram Dass took a picture of the politician and placed it on a table alongside some of his greatest heroes. Every time he paid homage to these heroes of his, he paid homage to the politician, too. It's not enough, you see, to not react with anger, it's important to get rid of the anger altogether.

I recently (today as a matter of fact) had a run-in with a guy who used to be a friend but in recent years he's taken to not liking me very much.

The man in question sent me a pretty insulting email, and he said things that really upset me. It was tempting to fly off the handle at him—my anger being based on the fear of being disrespected—but I held off from replying until I got my anger under control, which I did by reminding myself that I was being insulted because the guy in question had insecurities that he couldn't deal with. It took a lot of doing but I actually wrote that although I didn't agree with what he said, there would be no hard feelings from my side. I got another insulting email in return, but this time his words didn't anger me, mainly because I now knew that this was all about him, not me.

This man has presented me with a challenge. I've managed to choose not to get angry when this guy to insults me, but now I have to learn how to love him, and the only way in which I'll be able to do this is to love him for giving me this challenge. It's the only way I can grow. If I can love him for helping me live a more harmonious life, then I don't have to forgive him, I have to thank him, instead.

It might be a good idea for you to think about this concept of forgiveness and see if you can incorporate true forgiveness into your life by thanking those who make you angry. It's a tough one, that's for sure, but I'm finding that it's well worth the effort.

I'm turning the rest of this chapter over to you guys, more or less, by bringing you news and views on Mindful Bartending from bartenders all over the world. If you practice Mindful Bartending, and if bringing that practice into your craft has had an impact on your life, please drop me an email at gaz@ardentspirits.com and let me know about it.

Here's asking for peace, love, and huge tips cups during the coming year.

Puerto Rico's #1 Premium Rum

www.DonQ.com

Produced by Destilería Serrallés, Inc., Ponce, PR and distributed by Serrallés USA, LLC, Stamford, CT. Rum 20%, 21%, 30% & 40% ALC/VOL Don Q is best enjoyed in moderation.

OWN THE BEARD. BE THE LEGEND.

 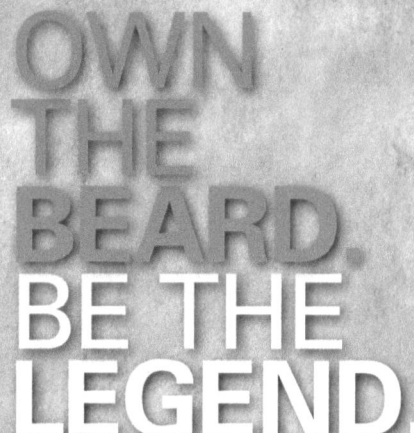

Black & Ginger Ale   Black & Stormy   Black & Cola

www.BlackBeardRum.com | www.facebook.com/BlackBeardSpicedRum

Produced by Destilería Serrallés, Inc., Ponce, PR and distributed by Serrallés USA, LLC, Stamford, CT. 43% ALC/VOL.

Mindful Bartender

Michael Stringer
Flip-It! Cocktail Mixologists, London, England

In late August, 2011, I received the following email from Michael:

> Hi Gaz:
>
> I have been reading your **Annual Manual** recently and must say how fantastic I am finding it.
>
> The whole section on Mindful Bartending, and being mindful in life generally is fascinating! I feel better already for using your techniques, such as meditation before a shift!
>
> I have even decided that when I compete tomorrow in the Brugal cocktail competition in London I am going to try something from your book, which I doubt has been done in a competition before. I am taking the advice from the quote by Harry Johnson in your book titled 'The greatest accomplishment of a bartender'.
>
> *["The greatest accomplishment of a bartender lies in exactly suiting his customer. This is done by inquiring what kind of a drink he wishes to have and how he desires to have it mixed . . . In following this rule, the barkeeper will soon gain the esteem and respect of his patrons."—The New and Improved Illustrated Bartenders' Manual or How to Mix Drinks of the Present Style: How to Mix Drinks of the Present Style by Harry Johnson, 1900.]*

I have decided that I will take a whole list of ingredients to the competition and just ask the judges what they want to taste. I will then proceed to make a drink based on what they have told me they like. I will let you know the outcome.

I hope to hear from you soon.

Michael Stringer, Director, Flip-It! Cocktail Mixologists

gaz sez: *Interesting, I thought. I asked Michael to keep me posted, and I soon heard from him again:*

Hi Gaz,

As promised I am letting you know how the competition went with Brugal last week.

I decided to use your technique of Mindful Bartending and just ask the judges to tell me a style of drink and what they wanted the drink to reflect. I then created a cocktail on the spot based on their preferences. Thanks to the advice in your book, I came in 1st place!

I am now through to the UK final being held at the boutique bar show!

gaz sez: *and after the finals, Michael wrote again to say:*

As promised, I am writing to keep you up to date with using your technique for my competitions.

Yesterday at the Boutique Bar Show, I competed in the UK finals of the Brugal cocktail competition.

Again using the same technique as before, inspired by yourself, I asked the judges what they would like me to make.

I asked the judges one question each:

What style of drink would you like?

What taste profile would you like in the drink? sweet or sour?

How would you like the drink presented? long? short? straight up?

And finally, how would you like the drink to make you feel? Any memories you would like provoked?

After assessing the judges' needs of a creamy, sweet, straight-up and winter drink bringing back Christmas memories, yet still bringing the overall flavours of the rum through.

I smiled and said thank you very much. I had a drink instantly. I have added my recipe below for you:

40ml Brugal Viejo Rum

20ml Chase Rhubarb liqueur

20ml Marzipan liqueur

Garnished with a cinnamon stick

I am very pleased to say that your technique works as I was placed 2nd in the UK!!

Thank you very much for opening my eyes to Mindful Bartending and I look forward to using it again in future!

gaz sez: *Thanks for letting us know about this, Michael, I hope that everyone reading this takes note. Here we have a case of Mindful Fulfillment being employed as a very successful tactic in a cocktail competition. It's so very important to be mindful of your guests' personal preferences, and when you take this to the street, bringing it into play during cocktail competitions, the rewards can be just fabulous.*

Mindful Bartender

Mihai Fetcu
Bistro de l'Arte, Brasov, Romania

gaz sez: *I received an unexpected email from Romania recently, and the writer, a bartender name Mihai, and I, got to exchanging a few ideas. I was so happy when I received the following missive from Mihai. Made my little heart glad, it did.*

...I saw your ad with the book and I wanted to get my hands on it, to see what mysteries are there hidden. Don't get me wrong, I have 4 of your other books, but this has something different, it has that ICHIE-GO ICHI-E :) if you know what I am saying . . . after reading the part with the mindful bartender I said to myself: this man is going crazy but I had to try it for myself to see if it works so I made [a] plan:

I live 20 minutes from the city center in my town where my work place is so I take every time a bus. Once I am in the bus, I go in the back and start thinking [about] the shift I am about to start. And I say in my mind loud and clear that: today I will have a great day, today I will do everything perfect, today I will not freeze, today I will help my colleagues with everything that I can, today I will be nice with everyone that I will encounter, today I will respect everyone, today my owners and my colleagues will be proud of me and I will be proud of them, today I am the smartest and the most beautiful in the world (not trying to get cocky but I read in a [sahaja-yoga] book that if you do that the universe will respond in a particular manner) and last but not the least, TODAY I WILL MAKE AT LEAST ONE PEOPLE HAPPY.

I finished reading your book like 2 weeks ago, and since then, I am more relaxed at work, the colleagues are nice with me (more than the usual), tips are greater and the owners are starting to give me more and more events and let me in charge of everything. This is very pleasant because I am working in this place for 1 month and the bartenders there are 41 and 42 years old with 10 and 11 years of being behind the stick :) and I am 23 years old. maybe the universe is starting to give me back something...maybe is karma, maybe is God..i don't know. . . I just know that I'm having the time of my life now (and I'm not using drugs–hee hee!).

gaz sez: *Here's a clear case of how setting positive intentions before going to work can pay off bigtime. By using his bus journey to work to have some positive thoughts about the people he works with, and his guests, Mihai ended up with more work, a happier work environment, and bigger tips. A practice such as this is so easy, and it can be so very rewarding.*

Mindful Bartender

Merlin Griffiths
Priory Tavern, London, England

gaz sez: *And we'll close this chapter with a missive I received from Merlin—he wrote it after reading part of the Mindful Bartending section in last year's Annual Manual. Here Merlin is referring to the part of that chapter in which I pointed out that nobody goes to a bar for a drink.*

Dear Gary,

I have also been preaching the mantra for several years now that no-one goes out "just for a drink" (unless you're an alcoholic, in which case you're just somebody I have a distaste for who can drink more than me). Even just 2 lads sitting at home going, "what the hell, let's just go for drink" actually mean, "I'm bored and restless, let's go out to the pub 'cause fun stuff happens over a pint or three…"

As a local landlord these days it's just more obvious too. People really are the lifeblood of any given premises, and as the current recession pushes many first time SME owners into the 'burbs/boondocks, this insight is thrown into stark relief.

Point being, as a pub owned by a one-time cocktail scene-ster, my staff all want the weird and wonderful drink knowledge gleaned from that world. But what I really want them to learn is the bigger picture of running bar; managing the atmosphere driven by love for your people that results in excellent anticipation and provision of guest needs. That and the money bit (can't be a bar if you don't make a profit too!).

gaz sez: *Nicely put, Merlin. It's always worth reminding ourselves that there's nothing wrong with making money, and if you fill your tip cup while truly being of service to your guests, you're making the world a better place.*

In Summation

The Mindful Bartending concept seems to be slowly catching on with bartenders all over the world, and it's something I intend to pursue again this year. If you didn't get last year's manual, in which I went into this concept in detail, you can still find the book at Mixellany.com, Amazon.com, and many more on-line sources. If you can't afford it, email me at gaz@ardentspirits.com and we'll work something out.

—gaz regan.

Chapter 2

Bartender Quotes of the Year

Martha, editor of this tome and my trusty sidekick here at Bar Rags, trolls the on-line bar-related scene nigh-on every day, and she's constantly letting me know about who has said what recently. She's a bit of a mind-reader is Ms. M, as I like to call her, so she knows what kind of stories will rock my boat and which stories will sink to the bottom of the Deep Blue, as it were. I'm not against helping shout out creative souls, for instance, but I'm more likely to enjoy highlighting bartenders who are thoughtful, caring, and sharing sorts—those who bring some aspect of mindfulness to our craft. You get the picture, right? In this section, we're bringing you a selection of what I believe to have been the best bartender quotes over the past twelve months or so. If I'm counting these correctly, I've selected eleven quotes from a pool of over 5,000 articles that we've linked to over the course of last year.

And I've commented on these quotes, too. That's another thing for which you have to thank Martha. It was her idea that

I throw my two cents into the ring here. When I pray, I try to end up by saying "and thanks for sending me a fabulous editor, God. You of all Beings know how much I need one . . ."

I've tried to give plenty of context so you can get the sense of each quote. If you'd like to see the full articles from which most of the quotes below were found, go to http://tinyurl.com/AM4Bartenders2012.

What is the Key to Happiness?

"There are always going to be things in life you don't like, things we have no control over, but we can control our attitude and perspective. If you can find a way to put a positive spin on things, you'll be happy."

–Sarah Daniel, **The Davenport**, Houston TX, USA
Source: Houston Press.com

gaz sez: *Sarah hits the nail on the head here, though it's a concept that can be pretty hard to grasp at times. Fact is that happiness and positive thinking are choices that we can make, even when things aren't going our way. We can choose to react to a situation with anger, or we can choose to react with love—our call. If we choose to look at situations in a positive light—f'rinstance, that guy just insulted me but I'm going to grab this opportunity to practice how not to let other people push my buttons—life can be so very sweet.*

I Like Making People Happy

Q: Is there something that you particularly like about bartending?"

A: I like making people happy. I like when a couple comes in, and they have a little problem and I can help them. Like George and Marie, they came in and they started fighting and she said, 'That's it!' but I helped them make peace. I told her, 'You are not enjoying your husband but think about people who are sick and in the hospital. You have to stay, say salud and forget.' They were hugging and kissing by the end of our talking."

–Lala Guirra, bartender, Conejito's Place,
Milwaukee WI, USA
Source: OnMilwaukee.com

gaz sez: *There's no feeling on earth that can compare to that lift you get when you put a smile on someone else's face. Being a bartender offers us a unique opportunity to touch other people's lives in this way. Good for you, Lala, for recognizing this. Lala is a perfect example of a Mindful Bartender who may not even realize she's being mindful. What she is doing is going with her instincts, her gut reaction, and as you can see, it pays off well for her.*

Look Them in the Eye

Q: What do you say to people who have had too much to drink?

A: "I will say different things depending on the situation, but it's most important to look them in the eye and make sure they are looking in your eye when you are talking to them. People usually hear more when you say things calmly than if you get aggressive or bark at them."

–Eric Reinstadtler, Tate's Craft Cocktails,
Winston-Salem NC, USA
Source: Winston-Salem Journal.

gaz sez: Eric nails this—connecting with others in a mindful way is all about eye contact, listening, and speaking to people with respect. When we look people in the eye we reach their souls. They know that we are truly listening to what they have to say, and this touches people in a very positive manner, mainly because it doesn't happen very often. Think about incorporating this practice into your craft behind the bar. If you do, I'm sure that you'll find that it pays off in so many ways your head will spin.

Each Person Is Smiling

The point is not how high the check average is or if they leave me 20 percent. The only point worth noticing is that they're at my bar and not someone else's. The only real thing that matters is if each person who sits at my bar is smiling. My profession is to make people happy . . . I love making a guest a drink that is original, thoughtful and that puts a smile on their face. I love to add ease to what might be a very hectic day. It's what I'm there for.

–Brian Melton, Tag Restaurant, Denver CO, USA
Source: Denver Westward Blogs (blogs.westword.com)

gaz sez: *Brian is obviously a bartender who recognizes what's truly important about our jobs. And that's not to the exclusion of being a great mixologist, either. I love his concept of "making a guest a drink that is original, thoughtful and that puts a smile on their face." There are so many ways in which we can make our guests happy, and it's up to us to try to figure out how best to put a smile onto each individual customer's face.*

Nerve Is a Tricky One

One of my mentors taught me that it takes four specific things to be a good bartender: charisma, uniqueness, nerve and talent. Charisma is something that will make someone come back and be a regular for you. Uniqueness ties right in to that—you don't want to be like every other bartender on the planet. If you stand out a bit, that will also make people come back and see you. Nerve is a tricky one; you have to not be afraid to be a bartender. There are some things that come with it, like cutting people off or jumping over the bar to do the Heimlich maneuver because someone is choking on a spring roll. You have to have confidence. Talent is thinking outside the box. Being able to make [your job] fun and keep it fresh.

–Ryan Huelsing , Bristol Seafood Grill, St. Louis MO, USA
Source: StLouis.Metromix.com

gaz sez: *I agree with all that Ryan has to say here, and the one thought that really jumps out at me is when he says, "you have to not be afraid to be a bartender." Being a bartender is similar* *in ways to being an actor. That's not to say that you are pretending to be someone else, far from it, but tending bar involves being watched, just like you're on a stage.*

Lots of bartenders love the "look-at-me" aspect of the job, and I certainly fit into that category, but that hasn't always been the case. As I wrote in the Mindful Bartending chapter of last year's Annual Manual, and which I go into in the Autobiography section of this book, when I first started tending bar in New York, in 1973, I was quite literally afraid of going behind the bar. I was afraid of making a fool out of myself, afraid of not having a smart answer when some of the guests would tease me, and I was afraid that nobody would take me seriously as a bartender. In short, I was afraid of being a bartender.

To remedy this fear, I indulged in a form of meditation that centered me and prepared me to "go on stage," each evening. It's part of the practice of Mindful Bartending. It's something I highly recommend, and if you're unsure how to start this kind of practice, I also highly recommend 8 Minute Meditation: Quiet Your Mind, Change Your Life *by Victor Davich.*

The Bad Girl of Bourbon

ESQ: So you weren't hired to wear a tank top and flirt with the customers?

JP: No, it wasn't sexy to be a bartender like it is today, and you certainly didn't call yourself a "mixologist." You were just a gal behind the bar who was slinging drinks and trying out recipes to make the whiskey taste better. I loved those tough old guys because they taught me how to make all the classics.

ESQ: Do they cut too many corners today?

JP: The old-timers taught me how to do it right: Don't use cheap vermouth, and use fresh juice, not bar mix. I grew up in the business when you made everything from scratch, but then that terrible period in America happened when the food industry went to hell and everything was pre-made and pre-mixed. But over the last twenty years, the food revolution came along and it has rolled over to the bar. The bartenders now have fresh, new ingredients to play with and to create these amazing drinks. It is so much fun being a bartender these days. I love to research and tinker with recipes. I think bartenders are developing cutting-edge beverage programs that match what the chefs are doing in the kitchen.

–Joy Perrine, Equus Restaurant
and Jack's Lounge, Louisville KY, USA
Source: Esquire.com

gaz sez: When I got behind the bar in the USA in 1973, what Joy describes here had already happened. We used commercial sweet-and-sour mix instead of lemon or lime juice, and there was very little by way of outside-the-box creativity going on. It's so fabulous for people of my generation to have witnessed the craft become so vital, to have seen true genius bartenders bringing us farm-to-glass potions, molecular marvels, and recipes worthy of Cordon-Bleu status. Jerry Thomas has been smiling from his grave these past few years.

It's a Perfect Day

gaz sez: *We have two quotes from the same article here. I love both of them, but the first one's a riot. This was bartender John Fausz's reply when he was asked about a book club that he started in his bar:*

It was kind of just a way to get through the winter months; to keep myself reading and active. I figured it would be fun to have a book club that you wouldn't invite your mom to. It's a good way to give people something to do at the bar that's not just getting drunk and talking to your friends. It's getting drunk and reading literature by drunk people!

gaz sez: *And we have to also bring you John's answer about what he loves most about tending bar:*

People; it's a social science kind of [thing]. I constantly get to see a good cross section of humanity and make friends every day. It's really nice, especially when I can match someone's mood [with a drink] or give them something they don't know they want and have them fall in love with it; it's a perfect day.

–John Fausz, The Royale, St. Louis MO, USA
Source: StLouis.Metromix.com

gaz sez: *John is my kind of guy. He's obviously a people person, he enjoys the creative process, and he doesn't take himself too very seriously. If I lived in St. Louis, I'd be a member of his book club, for sure.*

Put Your Personal Life at the Door

The hardest part is having to always be able to put your personal life at the door as soon as you walk in. That will always be the biggest thing at any job, but especially when you're in customer service. People don't come in here to listen to me bitch about my life. They come in here to relax.

—Devin Smith, The Union Cabaret & Grille,
Kalamazoo MI, USA
Source: Esquire.com

gaz sez: *As Devin says, this is, perhaps, one of the toughest things to do, and it's imperative that we do it. It's no good complaining about your life to people who might be at your bar so they can complain about theirs. And again I have to point towards meditation and centering yourself before your shift as a great way to accomplish this. Still your mind for a while and you'll find that you're able to set your intentions to being of service to your guests.*

A Very Quick Exit

He walked in by himself, stood there, and tried to order a drink while urinating. It was a very quick exit for him.

It's great that we're having better cocktails than ever. But three years from now, I could be pouring beers and still be totally happy.

–Mark Church, Wunder Bar at Grunauer,
Kansas City MO, USA
Source: Esquire.com

gaz sez: *When I started tending bar again in 2004, holding weekly "organized chaos" gatherings at my local, Painter's Tavern in Cornwall-on-Hudson, New York, one of the owners, Pete Buttiglieri, saw my cocktail list before the first night and he warned me that he wasn't sure how many of my "weird cocktails" we could sell in our neck of the woods.*

"It doesn't matter, Pete," I said. "What matters is that we have fun and we make some money. If they drink beer and wine I'll be quite happy, just so long as we have fun and make money."

And that seems to be Mark Church's views on the subject, too. I like that sort of bartender because it proves to me that they are, above all else, a bartender. What kind of drinks you serve is not the point. The point is that you serve.

Q: How did you decide to donate half of your tips to Movember[1]?

A: It's not that I don't think that the way they do it is good—the reason I'm doing this is because of what they're doing. I just wanted to take it on to myself and do something. It feels good. It's kind of greedy in that way because it feels good.

—Fritz Fulton, Woodlands Tavern, Columbus OH, USA
Source: ColumbusAlive.com

gaz sez: *"It's kind of greedy in that way because it feels good," says Fritz. And I know exactly what he's talking about. Chances are that you know what he's talking about, too. If you don't though, I'm going to ask you to think about trying a little experiment.*

Every night for a month, take five percent of your tip cup and donate it to charity. You can give it to a homeless person on the street, you can drop it into the collection plate at your place of worship, you can stick it into the hand of someone you know who is down on his or her luck, or you can write a check to a charity of your choice.

See how good you feel after you do this. Write to me at gaz@ardentspirits.com after you do this and tell me all about it. You can do it again next month if you wish, or you can drop the concept

---

1   Every November, Movember is responsible for the sprouting of moustaches on thousands of men's faces, both in the US and around the world. With their Mo's, these men raise vital funds and awareness for men's health, specifically prostate cancer and other cancers that affect men.

and write it off as a lesson learned if it doesn't work for you. We're talking just five percent of your tip-cup here. It's not going to break the bank, you know, and I predict that you'll better understand what Fritz means when he says that his giving is sort of a greedy thing to do. When you give something away, you're giving it to yourself, you see. Try it out and see if you understand what I'm talking about.

Tonight Your Name Is Vino-Not

I love my job. That's the only reason I do it. Anyone can be a bartender, but if you don't have love and passion, the drink is going to taste awful. I mean, everyone's got problems. There's a trash can outside that door. When I come in here, that's where I leave my trash.

I had a famous gentleman come in here. He asked my name, I told him, Dino. He said 'No, tonight your name is Vino.' I said, 'No, it's Dino.' He throws a $100 bill on the bar. 'Say your name is Vino.' I said no. Throws $200 down. 'Your name is Vino.' I said no. He throws $300, $400, $500... I said 'You can drop $1000, you can't buy me.' Guy couldn't believe it. It's principle. I have pride. Who are you, thinking you can come in here, and make me dance? It's the principle. When he was leaving, he said 'Look at all my buddies around me. I can buy them for $100, but I couldn't buy you for $500 for just changing your name. I respect you.' I said 'I respect you too, have a good night'... Celebrity, lawyer or construction worker, when they get drunk, it's the same thing."

–Dino, bartender at Bistro Lancaster
at the Lancaster Hotel, Houston TX, USA
Source: HoustonPress.com.

gaz sez: *NEVER let yourself get bought by a customer. Being bought is not the same as being of service. It's succumbing to blackmail. And blackmailers always want more once they discover that you'll bow to their wants. It's one of the worst mistakes you'll ever make. Thanks, Dino, for bringing this up. It's a great point you make.*

NO-NOS FROM UNCLE HARRY

Bartenders should not, as some have done, have a toothpick in their mouth, clean their fingernails while on duty, smoke, spit on the floor, or have other disgusting habits.

—*New and Improved Illustrated Bartender's Manual* by Harry Johnson, 1900.

THE QUINTESSENTIAL BARTENDER

The quintessential bartender has seen it all, can handle it all and always has an answer for everything, even if he or she really doesn't.

—Heather Bradwin, former bartender, Fond du Lac WI, USA, Fdlreporter.com, July 28, 2010.

Chapter 3

Bartenders' Bartenders of the Year

It's true that I travel all over the world and I get to meet hundreds of bartenders each year, but it's seldom that I have time to really watch them work. As a result, I really need help in order to bring you a good representation of the best of the best bartenders out there. This section, then, is dedicated to bartenders whom I have never met but are good enough at their jobs to spur their fellow bartenders on to write to me about them.

It was pretty tough to filter through the 500+ suggestions I received, trying to figure out who to feature, and who not to feature, but for various and sundry reasons, all of which will become clear to you as you read on, I finally narrowed it down to the following nine bartenders. Congratulations to one and all.

Here's what's up, then, with this year's list of Bartenders' Bartenders. (These are in no particular order.)

Ben Simpson

Coco at the Roxy, Wellington, New Zealand

Jonny McKenzie of the Hawthorn Lounge in Wellington wrote to tell me about Ben, and more than a few others have since said some luverly things about the lad. Here's what Jonny wrote:

> I would like to put forward Ben Simpson who was once the manager of a bar called Motel in Wellington, New Zealand. Ben has been a leader, teacher, creator, and book of knowledge for young and old bartenders of Wellington & New Zealand.
>
> He grew Motel from strength to strength continually winning local competitions and representing New Zealand in many other cocktail related competitions. He is the proud creator of Gun Powder Rum, which I hope you have had the pleasure of tasting via Jacob Briars or Angus Winchester.
>
> Ben has always been incredibly humble in his approach to the cocktail world but has gained much respect in his abilities. Therefore may I please recommend Ben Simpson as a Bartender for you to research for your **Annual Manual**.

gaz sez: *Jonny wasn't the only bartender who had great things to say about Ben. The following came in from India:*

> Where to start with describing a man who is equal parts brilliant at everything he turns his hand to with the driest of wits. Self-confessed Modesty Blaise fanatic, steam-punk purist, pirate, buccaneer and outstanding gentleman with a passion, intelligence and dedication

that has seen him create one of the most talked about products in bartending circles since St. Germain popped out of a pretty French orchard.

I fondly remember [Ben] hand-typing the menus for New Zealand's first true speakeasy, Motel, letting me rest my eyes at the bar after being over-served by his enthusiastic bar team and for the never ending shots of Fernet Branca.

–Tim Etherington Judge, India.

gaz sez: *and from the one and only Jacob Briars:*

Benedict 'BH' Simpson is a unique bartender and one of the very finest people in an industry filled with great characters. His soon-to-be-very-famous Smoke'n'Oakum Gunpowder Rum is becoming a cult product around the world, while in his hometown of Wellington, he is loved as an unshowy barkeep with keen intelligence, wit and a passion for history (but he is no slave to it). Ben is a wonderful mentor to young bartenders in New Zealand, an inspiration to budding bartender-businesspeople, and I always look forward to pulling up a barstool in front of him.

–Jacob Briars

gaz sez: *Congratulations, Ben. You're obviously a fabulous Bartenders' Bartender. I love that Jonny noted your humility, and that, combined with your propensity to teach others, makes you stand out in the crowd. And the fact that you even created your own brand of rum, described on the rum's Facebook page as: "A rum of rich flavour and history augmented by no-fuss, old-style, blunderbuss black gunpowder," seals the deal. Hopefully we'll bend elbows together one of these fine days.*

MANDARINE
NAPOLÉON

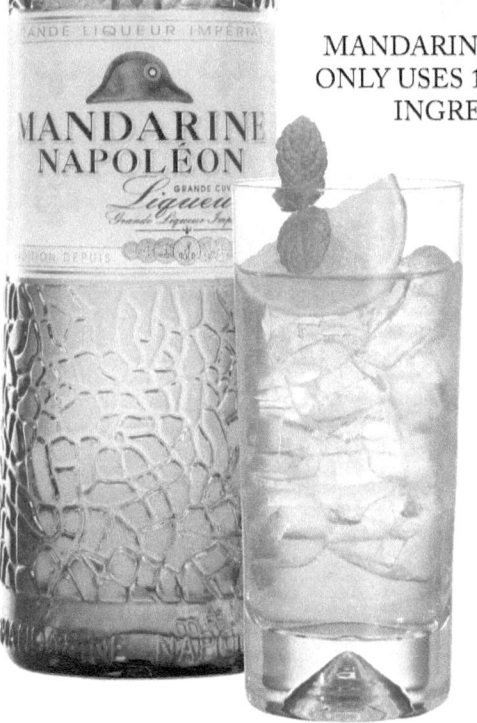

MANDARINE NAPOLÉON IS BASED ON A BLEND OF DISTILLATE OF THE FINEST ESSENTIAL OILS OF MANDARINES AND AGED COGNAC FROM THE GRAND REGION OF COGNAC.

FOUR SPICES RICH IN ESSENTIAL OILS AND AROMATIC PRINCIPLES AND TWO PLANTS ACCOMPLISH THIS UNIQUE COMPOSITION OF FLAVOURS.

MANDARINE NAPOLÉON ONLY USES 100% NATURAL INGREDIENTS.

for the facts **drinkaware.co.uk**

George Restrepo

Coppelia Club, Barcelona, Spain

Moira López wrote to tell me about George Restrepo, and Moira is likely just a little biased since she's married to the man, but nonetheless, this guy stood tall when his credentials were scrutinized, and I don't think there's any doubt that George Restrepo is, indeed, a Bartenders' Bartender. Here's an edited version of the email that Moira sent:

> Dear gaz, I've been thinking a lot about answering this email and helping you in your data collection, certainly something really hard to do! The thing is that I want to recommend my husband, so I wasn't sure if it "politically correct" to do so. But I thought 'Ok, he is my husband, but he is also my business partner, and one of the best bartenders too!' So, I will do it ;)
>
> George is a versatile creative person, by definition. He has been working hard in the creation of cocktails in the past years and this activity is something he has integrated to his own life, living it as part of his daily routine. Every situation could be a possibility; a new ingredient is a new idea, each lesson is an opportunity. The result is living with this philosophy where the perspective is always directed by this mission: to Create, to Innovate, to Share.
>
> Being in one of the Cocktail Premium Bar in Barcelona, gives him the opportunity to explore as I mentioned before but also to be near to famous figures. This was the case with the singing pop star Shakira. He created a special cocktail for Shakira named "Magia" (Magic, this is the name of her first album). She loved it!"

gaz sez: *Thanks, Moira! What clinched this one for me was George's mission: to Create, to Innovate, to Share. He certainly sounds like my kind of bartender.*

Daniel Bovey

Sahara Bar, Reading, England

Rick James Williams of the Sahara Bar put Daniel's name forward as a Bartenders' Baretender via email. Here's a lightly edited version of what he wrote:

> Hi Gaz, In response to your article in Imbibe mag last month, I'd like to put forward my General Manager, [Daniel Bovey]. Having worked with him for approximately 12 months now, he has in this time been through to the UK Chartreuse finals (2011), the final round of the Bacardi Legacy comp (2010) and competed in numerous other events including brands such as Trois Rivieres rhum, Jack Daniel's, Russian Standard vodka and Grand Marnier. He was runner up for Grand Marnier, and is being sent to Cognac this month. Not only that, he and a fellow bartender recently came 3rd in the Grand Marnier Grand Bal in London, runner up only to the Savoy and the Playboy Club (Salvatore Calabrese). He has also won the Chambord Rendezvous competition for his apéritif "Auld Alliance", has just won a Bacardi Oakheart mixing & flair competition, and is through to the finals of Bacardi Legacy once again this year.
>
> It's inspirational to work under someone with such a genuine passion for the industry and all sides involved in it. The main thing however is that he is a thoroughly nice chap, and has a great sense of humour. Being professional and still approachable, and with the knowledge and skill to deliver great drinks time and time again is an endearing weapon in his arsenal, and he will most certainly go far.

gaz sez: *The last paragraph sealed it for me. That, plus watching him in action on YouTube. Daniel comes across really well. His El Momento Perfecto, a drink he created for the Bacardi Legacy Competition in 2011, will be included in this year's 101 Best New Cocktails. Don't miss it!*

PART 2 • THE MINDFUL BARTENDER

Daisuki Onishi

Twilight, Beijing, China & Apothecary, Beijing, China

Paul Mathew, co-owner of The Hide cocktail bar in London, is based in Beijing; he writes for *DRiNK* Magazine (Associate Editor) and works various liquor companies as a trainer and an occasional brand ambassador. He also consults for bars in China, and occasionally works behind the stick at a steak restaurant/cocktail bar called Flamme. He wrote to recommend Daisuke Oniski at Twilight and Apothecary in Beijing. Paul writes of Daisuki:

> He is co-owner/bartender in these places and is excellent. He is Japanese/English and has a very classic Japanese approach to cocktails, but with an English/American bartender's desire to try out new things and experiment with flavours and brands.

> **gaz sez:** *I'm fascinated by the mix of Eastern and Western styles that's going down behind bars all over the world these days, and it sounds as though Daiskue has pretty much nailed the balance on this front. I believe that it's advantageous to all of us to learn from each other, and to incorporate whatever innovations feel right to us into our own personas behind the bar. Now if I can just persuade someone to take me to Beijing...*

PART 2 • THE MINDFUL BARTENDER

Tim D Philips

Ivy, Level 6, Sydney, Australia

Ben Shipley, a Creative Director for the Australian branch of Hill and Knowlton, worked for 42 Below in China and New Zealand, both before and after the sale to Bacardi, and he writes about drinking and hospitality in his blog, everydaydrinking.wordpress.com.

"I haven't put in the years behind the stick, [but] I can turn out a drink and know the dull ache you have the morning after you've turned out a thousand drinks," he says.

Ben went on to recommend Tim D Philips, a bartender who works at Ivy, Level 6, in Sydney:

> [He] has worked at Milk & Honey, was UK Bartender of the Year in 2009, has magnificent chat and has furnished me some of the finest beverages I've ever been lucky enough to imbibe. You might get a chance to meet him in Delhi, he is representing Australia in the World Class Finals.
>
> **gaz sez:** *I did, indeed, meet Tim in India, and a damned fine bartender he is, too. Tim is one of those "cheeky-chappie" sorts who's always sporting a winning smile, and he's quick with a quip when the moment's right, too. I'll bet that Tim is the reason that lots of the customers at his bar go back there time and time again.*

Timo Siitonen

A21, Helsinki, Finland

Kimmo Aho, a Senior Lecturer at the JAMK University of Applied Sciences in Finland, wrote to say:

> The best bartender Finland has to offer is Timo Siitonen. Timo started his career in London 1999, moved back to Helsinki 2005, opened a bar A21 in 2007, published a bartender's manual in 2009, was voted to be a best bartender in Finland in 2010. Ever since the opening the A21 has been regarded as a best cocktail bar in Finland and it also became the best bar in worldsbestbar.com in 2009, currently holding the position 10. The reason why I think Timo should be noticed is the fact that he simply brought the Finnish bar culture into the 21th century and is a role model for the next generation of bartenders in Finland.

> **gaz sez:** *In London it's Dick Bradsell, in New York it's Dale DeGroff, and obviously, in Helsinki it's Timo Siitonen who has brought the cocktail culture up to date and given Finnish bartenders something to aim for. Well done, Timo.*

Dave Newman

Nobu, Waikiki HI, USA

Mike Bourroughs, an ex-bartender living in San Francisco, wrote to tell us about a bartender in Hawaii:

> I [found] the most amazing bartender on a return trip to Hawaii where my wife and I had our honeymoon 25 years ago. We stayed at the Halekulani hotel in Waikiki where we had an amazing time and some great cocktails at a Dale DeGroff re-done bar, called Lewers Lounge. One of the bartenders there sent us across the street to the bar inside of Nobu. Here we were blown away with the bar manager Dave Newman. I have never seen a bartender make cocktails the way he does. Basically [he] interviewed us for a minute finding out what we liked, then went about creating original cocktails for each of us. I myself love the classics, I could be perfectly happy drinking a Manhattan or Negroni, while my wife prefers things a little lighter and more citrus based. We went to Nobu two times while we were in Waikiki, each night having 4-5 cocktails each. It started to become a game with us, we knew it would be a matter of time before Dave would make us something that we didn't enjoy. Each round of drinks was amazing. Something like 17 original cocktails and only one that he made from a recipe that he didn't create. We didn't try any of the drinks on the menu, but the people sitting around us seemed to enjoy those as well. Taking the time to describe each drink and the process that he used to create them made the experience over the top. So many homemade syrups, bitters and combinations that I previously would have thought wouldn't work, simply did. Dave told us that he has one goal when creating a new drink and that is balance. He would use a straw to taste every drink, then add what he felt would bring the drink into balance. Watching this process was almost

as much fun as taking the first sip of each new drink. I could not believe that he was not writing down any of the drink recipes as he created them. He said that he tries to make each drink made this way as an original, I wanted to strangle him and force him to record the recipes. Some of these drinks are the best I have ever had and all of them were great. The idea that I can never have them again is a tragedy. When I saw your article looking for the best of the best, I thought that you had to meet this guy. For selfish reasons I thought maybe you could get some of these recipes on paper and I could try to recreate them down the road. I know you were looking for more bartenders out of the US to showcase, but Hawaii is almost like another place. Anyway, even if this doesn't fit in with what you were looking for, he is one to watch.

gaz sez: *Sometimes it is about the drinks! And Mike does us all a service by reminding us what Dave Newman demonstrates: that the quality of the drinks we serve is important. It's all a question of being able to balance our skills so that we can be complete bartenders, with the capabilities of wearing one of myriad hats when the opportunity presents itself.*

Simon McGoram

Porteno, Sydney, Australia
&
Gardel's Bar, Sydney, Australia

Edward Washington, Deputy Editor at *Australian Bartender* magazine, wrote to recommend Simon McGoram, a Kiwi who also works at the magazine, and a man who made me run upstairs for a meeting with Dave Spanton when I was Down Under a few years back, as a Bartenders' Bartender. Despite the 100-meter dash, I have to agree with Edward. Here's what he wrote:

> He is the Drinks Editor here at Australian Bartender, [and Simon] also tends the bar at the top-notch Porteno and Gardel's Bar (at Porteno) in Sydney. If you're looking for a bartender with the right attributes, then he is certainly your man. Apart from an encyclopaedic knowledge of all things bar/ beverage related he has knife edge wit (and opinion), intelligence and manners that would make him not out of place tending bar in the 1920s. In fact I often tell him he's a colourful character, straight from the Great Gatsby era of before. If you want bartenders who can make their own Smokey Islay Caramel Fudge, and serve it with an equally impressive cocktail, then he should most certainly be included.

gaz sez: *I know Simon, Met him in Oz few years ago when* Australian Bartender *magazine flew me down there for their bar show. It's as simple as this: Simon is the real deal. He has his priorities straight, he knows that service is where it's at, and he's also always on top of every little detail. The organization at that bar show was second to none, and although I'm aware that he wasn't the only one making sure that everything went down well, I also know that he had a couple of dozen balls in the air at any given moment, and not one of them ever hit the ground. Well done, Simon.*

Fernando Del Diego

Del Diego, Madrid, Spain

Neyah White, the famed San Francisco bartender who now works as a brand ambassador for Suntory, wrote to recommend Fernando Del Diego as a Bartenders' Bartender. And given what Neyah wrote, Fernando certainly deserves mention here:

> Have you been to Madrid recently? A few years ago, Fernando Del Diego left his hotel bar career and opened Del Diego with his two sons. Either of them qualify for the top slot in any serious cocktail bar, but they defer to their father, giving him the center well and flanking him as support on the two side wells of their good-bar. He wears a suit while they work in their shirt sleeves (although, he still seems to out produce them).
>
> Two summers ago I had the pleasure of going there twice. On the second visit it was a little less busy and Don Fernando came over to thank me for coming in again and to chat. He had picked up that I was a bartender somehow and when I told him I was from San Francisco he asked me about my bar and what the program was like. He even asked me for some recipes. I was pretty flattered and faltered a bit so I asked for some paper so I could write some stuff down as a stalling move. He gave it to me and left to make a drink. What he came back with surprised the hell of me. Knowing I was from the States, he grabbed for the Havana Club immediately and shook up a Piña Colada with a local coconut syrup. It was fantastic.
>
> Anyway, this guy is a classic and watchinga career barman working alongside his sons, something so few of us get to experience, just remarkable. Their program is firmly classic, based on quality bottles and technique with little bits of creative flair added here and there. Mostly, the

Del Diegos are gentlemen, hardworking and caring and theirs is easily the best bar in Madrid.

gaz sez: *If Neyah White shouts you out, you must be a fabulous bartender, and Neyah went to a lot of trouble to make sure I knew exactly how much he loved the way in which Fernando Del Diego handles himself. (For those of you who might not be aware of this, Havana Club isn't available in the States, and that's why Neyah was impressed that Fernando grabbed a bottle of this fabulous rum to make his Piña Colada.)*

In Summation

This is the first time I'm featuring "Bartenders' Bartenders" in the *Annual Manual*, and the response I got to requests for you guys to let me know who you admire most made my little heart glad. Thanks so much.

If you have suggestions for people who you think deserve mention in next year's Annual Manual, please drop me a line at gaz@ardentspirits.com and tell me all about them.

Ta Muchly,

gaz

A VERY PASSABLE GAME OF RUGBY FOOTBALL

We stayed up every night at ceilidhs singing songs and drinking the malt until dawn. According to the final counting we [4 people] drank twenty-eight bottles of single malt in the four days we were there, and on the Saturday morning I caught the boat and train back to Edinburgh and played a very passable game of Rugby football at Murrayfield that afternoon.

—*A Drop o' Malt* by Iain Crawford. Found in *The Compleat Imbiber* (4), 1961, Cyril Ray, editor.

Chapter 4

Fabulous Bartender Awards

I've selected nineteen bartenders to be recipients of this year's Fabulous Bartender Awards, and each of them will be getting a Gazzer 2012 bobblehead to put in the attic, or whatever it is you do with such stuff.

Big thanks to Pernod-Ricard USA for holding the Gazzer Award Show at the Parkside Lounge on East Houston Street in Manhattan during the Manhattan Cocktail Classic in May this year. You guys are Fabulous in your own right.

Why did I choose who I chose this year? Myriad reasons, and I go into details about why I chose everyone in each case, so you'll know why I chose these guys as you read about this year's recipients. I also asked each of the bartenders chosen this year a bunch of questions so we can get to know them a little better, and I think that, when you read some of their answers, you'll understand better why they were picked. You can also learn an awful lot from these questionnaires, so please pay attention—these guys know what they're talking about.

I will also let you know that not all of these Fabulous Bartenders do much bartending these days. I chose them not because of their skills behind the bar—though each of them have been pretty much masters of the craft—but because they have left the bar and built successful bar-related businesses for themselves. Rather than add a category of Fabulous Entrepreneurs for these people, I realized that even though they may not work behind the stick much (if at all), each one still walks the path of the bartender and has the soul of a bartender—and I can think of no higher compliment.

They are listed in alphabetical order by first name. Congratulations to each and every one of the bartenders listed here.

THE BLESSING OF SIR WILFRID LAWSON

His first experiment was at the Astor House bar in New York, when he went in for a brandy cocktail. To see the waiter mix the cocktail was a sight to remember. It was like conjuring. He dabbed first one ingredient and then another into a glass, then poured it out into another glass, infused an effervescing element, poured it backward and forward until it assumed a beautiful froth-like form, and finally served it up with a handful of ice. Barnacles described it as nectar, and, as he quaffed it, invoked the blessing of Sir Wilfrid Lawson [a British temperance leader]."

—Two Sides of the Atlantic
by James Burnley, 1880.

Adam Elmegirab

Aberdeen, Scotland

gaz sez: *I've never met Adam, though we came damned close to bumping into each other at the Berlin Bar Convent in 2011. Alas, divine intervention made it so that I had to buy my own drinks in Germany rather than cadging them from the wee Scot who has become an email pal of sorts.*

Adam is quite obviously quite the entrepreneur, and that's why I've chose to award him a Gazzer this year, but business skills aren't the only thing that have impressed me about Adam Elmegirab. The lad quite obviously has the heart and the soul of a true bartender. His tweets and his Facebook postings make that plain to see. He's thoughtful, he cares about the craft, and, perhaps most importantly, Adam is a great communicator. He knows how to grab people's attention. And he manages to do it with a wink and a nod so I get the impression that he doesn't take himself too very seriously. I love that in a bartender. It's something I strive toward.

Having said that, I urge you to read Adam's answers in the following Q & A section. He seems to have to ability to not take himself too seriously, while at the same time taking his businesses very seriously indeed. There's great advice from Adam here. I hope you don't miss it.

Business Name & Address: Evo-lution / Dr. Adam Elmegirab's Bitters, Margaret Place, Aberdeen, Scotland, AB10 7GB

Q: How long did you work behind the bar?

A: I started in 2001 and worked full-time for a little over 10 years. Though bartending is no longer my main job I still run regularly run events and will be found behind a bar somewhere every fortnight or so.

Q: Name the bars where you worked, and what cities they are in.

A: The first bar I stepped behind was TGI Fridays in Aberdeen in 2001. Since then I've worked for and with a number of others—in various capacities such as bartender, trainer and consultant—namely at Dusk, Mim, Ninety-Nine Bar & Kitchen, Yatai, Orchid, Carmelite Hotel and Fusion Bar & Bistro, RGU Union, DUSA and Sinclair's.

Q: What did you love, and what did you hate, about bartending?

A: The only things that have ever really gotten on top of me in my bartending career were the long hours and difficult guests who had little-to-no manners. I also get frustrated at bartenders who can't see the opportunities that bartending presents them. It is such an amazing industry with so many career opportunities.

As for what I loved, there was so much, to the point that I miss being a full-time bartender. If I was pushed for a specific answer I would probably go with the freedom and creativity that bartending gives you, meeting new people on a regular basis, and knowing that no two days would be the same.

Q: How did you start up your present business or businesses?

A; Evo-lution grew out of the increasing interest and demand in all things cocktails. It was around 2005 that I was regularly being asked to bartend at private events, and around this same time where I was approached to consult for a new bar that was opening in my hometown.

Seeing a potential opportunity I decided to invest in a bunch of business cards, a website and a new computer. This was where the consultancy, training and events side of things was born.

Dr. Adam Elmegirab's Bitters was a little different, though I guess it came about because of the doors I'd opened with my previous work in the industry. Intrigue into how the drinks from Jerry Thomas' 1862 *Bartender's Guide* would have tasted, compared to how we make them now, prompted me to start The Jerry Thomas Project. This in turn led me down a path of recreating Jerry's favoured bitters, Boker's, which had been lost around the time of Prohibition. After successfully reformulating a few bottles for myself I started being bombarded by bartenders and enthusiasts from all over the globe. One thing led to another and I now have a portfolio containing four different types of bitters and am in the top five bitters producers in the world.

Q: Do you think that being a bartender helped to prepare you for the work you do now?

A: Definitely, if there's one thing above all others, bartending really taught me the art of when to listen and when to speak. As an old football manager once shouted at me when I was younger, "You've got two f*cking ears and one f*cking mouth, use them in that proportion."

With that in mind, after the cocky young bartender phase that we all go through, I quickly realized that for me to progress I wasn't to be afraid of asking questions, no-one has the answer to everything so there's nothing wrong with asking the right questions of the right people. By the same token I learnt not to be afraid of voicing my opinion when necessary. As time has gone on I've realized I have increasing experience and knowledge to share. You also learn that you can learn from everything around you, this is how we progress as individuals and as a collective.

Q: What advice would you give to bartenders who might try to get into similar businesses as yours?

A: Adopt the same approach as you would when creating a cocktail for a competition or to feature on a menu. Carry out your due-diligence, research as much as you can, don't just jump in without testing the water, decide on a clear, concise concept, seek opinions from the right people, take inspiration but don't plagiarize, try not to over-complicate it, and ensure that what you're offering is tailored to suit your market demographic.

Q: Anything else you'd like to add?

A: I'll take a Martinez please. Old Tom Gin, Italian vermouth, maraschino and Boker's Bitters.

Adam Seger

HUM Spirits, Chicago IL, USA

gaz sez: *I've known Adam since the mid-1990s, if memory serves. He was working the Seelbach Hotel in Louisville, Kentucky, and Mardee and I had just published The Book of Bourbon and we were staring work on New Classic Cocktails. Adam had uncovered the recipe for the Seelbach Cocktail in the hotel's archives, and he was keeping the recipe close to his vest. We came to an agreement without much ado, though: He would tell us the recipe if we published it in our upcoming book He did, and we did, and now the drink is known worldwide.*

Adam's a real go-getter. He's always got something new up his sleeve, and as co-creator of Hum, an infused rum-based liqueur, he's more than earned the title of Fabulous Entrepreneur this year. Let's hear what Adam has to say for himself:

Q: How long did you work behind the bar?

A: Twenty-one years.

Q: Name the bars where you worked, and what cities they are in.

A: Regent Lounge, Statler Hotel at Cornell Hotel School, Ithaca NY; Old Seelbach Bar, The Oakroom and Max's Bar at The Seelbach Hotel, Louisville KY; Nacional 27, Chicago, IL.

Q: What do you love, and what do you hate, about bartending?

A: I love the unedited relationship between the bartender and the guest where you can customize exactly what is going to make your guests' evening. I hate fruit flies.

Q: What advice would you give to people who want to become bartenders?

A: If you love making people happy, you get off on eating and drinking well and you find physically challenging work satisfying, GO FOR IT. If not, grab a barstool in front of the stick and keep us in business.

Q: In what direction do you see the craft going in the next 5 years?

A: More of a connection between the bartender and the kitchen and the bartender and local farmers.

Q: How did you start up your present business or businesses?

I had enough guests encouraging me to take all my homemade things behind the bar and turn them into a product they could enjoy themselves at home or at other restaurants. So, I brought a sample of HUM to Tales of the

Cocktail in 2007 and tasted it with our 1st distillers Sonja and Derek Kassebaum. The rest is history.

Q: Do you think that being a bartender helped to prepare you for the work you do now?

A: I would not have been able to create HUM and grow it organically had I not been a bartender. I also continue to bartend as a guest and trainer extensively, making cocktails for people about 3 nights a week somewhere.

Q: What advice would you give to bartenders who might try to get into similar businesses as yours?

A: Get an attorney you trust, a financier you trust, read your operating agreement before signing it and make a solid, detailed plan and budget. Then double the $ you think you need, double the time you think it will take, and get started ASAP. Overnight success takes about 10-20 years.

Q: Anything else you'd like to add?

A: "Drink Like You Eat" and you cannot go wrong. Contact Adam Seger if you need help [getting a new business off the ground]: 312.213.4878, adam@adamseger.com. I have been blessed to have Gary Regan, Dale Degroff, Max Allen and Francesco LaFranconi as my mentors and am happy to give back unselfishly as they have taught me.

Ago Perrone

Connaught Hotel, London, England

gaz sez: *I first met Ago in June, 2006, when I was visiting the London Bar Show for the very first time. He was at work behind the stick at Montgomery Place, and he made me the very best Martinez I'd ever had in my life. I can think of only two or three drinks that have been so well crafted that they bowled me over at first sip, and Ago's Martinez was one of them. His cocktailian skills, though, have nothing to do with the reason that I selected him to be a Fabulous Bartender this year.*

If you've ever met Ago Perrone you'll have noticed that his impish grin is the first thing that strikes you about the man, and I'm sure that you'll agree with me when I say that his warmth is palpable. He is the epitome of hospitality. There's something else fabulous about Ago, though, and there's a chance you might not know this. What Ago gets right that so many of us get wrong is that he treats absolutely everyone he meets in exactly the same way. As warm as he is to you, is as warm as he is to everyone else in the room. Whether you're wearing a tux or a T-shirt, Ago's welcome will be exactly the same. Ago is a Fabulous Bartender. Let's take a look at what he has to say for himself.

PART 2 • THE MINDFUL BARTENDER

Q: How long have you worked behind the bar?

A: Thirteen years.

Q: Name the bars where you worked, and what cities they are in.

A: L'isola che non c' e', Monza (Italy); 3f American Bartender School, Milan (Italy); Salvador and Amanda, London; Dusk, London; Montgomery Place, London; The Connaught Bar, London.

Q: What do you love, and what do you hate, about bartending?

A: Love: In order to push your creativity you need to be aware of cultures, flavors, history, geography—and then mix them up in one shaker. And our guests also play a very important role because they give us suggestions and inspiration as well.

Hate: bar owners who don't understand the full meaning of bartending; innovation, quality, financial aspects, technical skills and ergonomics of the bar that improve service and operation—all those things are linked to each other, and without just one of them, the bartender's job is much more difficult.

Q: What advice would you give to people who want to become bartenders?

A: Believe your dreams and follow them using your own ideas and personality. It doesn't matter what you do, but how you do it. You don't have to learn complicated methodology, or use hard-to-find ingredients—what really counts is your own personal style.

Q: In what direction do you see the craft going in the next 5 years?

A: I think that we'll see a fusion of service skills, creativity, and understanding flavors, just as it was 150 years ago when bartenders such as Harry Johnson and Jerry Thomas started to write the first bartender's manuals.

Q: Anything else you'd like to add?

A: Straight up with style and don't forget the smile!

Alex Kammerling

Kamm & Sons, London, England

gaz sez: *I don't know Alex well at all. In fact we've met only once, but his name comes up over and over again, and his Ginseng Spirit, flavored with 45 botanicals, including four varieties of ginseng, has become immensely popular since its launch. We're still waiting for it in the USA, and hopefully we'll get it sooner rather than later.*

Here's a bio of Alex—he sent it to me on request—so you can get a handle on his background:

Alex Kammerling has been working within the drinks industry for 18 years having started his career as a humble bartender. Alex has worked in cafés, wine bars, cocktail bars, hotel bars and restaurants from London to Sydney via Hong Kong.

For the last 10 years Alex has been running his own drinks consultancy, working in the top of the industry with leading brands such as Grey Goose, Stolichnaya, Courvoisier, Schweppes and Bombay Sapphire. He has held training sessions and given presentations to thousands of bartenders on spirits, cocktails and service skills from Edinburgh to Montego Bay, managed events such as Elton John's White Tie and Tiara party to the Prada store opening in Paris. In his time as a bartender Alex has made drinks for the world's most successful artists, actors, fashion designers, models, rock stars and royalty and has created hundreds of contemporary classic cocktails and judged some internationally recognized cocktail competitions such as the 42 Below World Cup in New Zealand.

Alex has also been writing articles for leading drinks and consumer magazines for over 9 years and has had a number of appearances on Television. In 2004 his own cocktail book, entitled 'Blend me, Shake me', was published by BBC books. Alex has recently left his role as Brand Ambassador for Grey Goose vodka to launch his own brand 'Kamm & Son's – Ginseng Spirit'. He is 36 and lives in North London.

Q: How long did you work behind the bar?

A: Full time for 5 years, part time/events 7 years.

Q: Name the bars where you worked, and what cities they are in.

A: 69 Colebrook Row, London; Detroit Bar, London; Shermans, Hong Kong; Bar Georgio, Sydney

Q: What did you love, and what did you hate, about bartending?

A: Loved the creativity, the sociability, the music and the excitement. Not so keen on late hours and bad pay.

Q: How did you start up your present business or businesses?

A: With a lot of perseverance and patience. After having been a creative drink-maker and an ambassador for a number of global brands I felt like I had enough connections, experience and vision to produce my own unique drinks brand.

Q: Do you think that being a bartender helped to prepare you for the work you do now?

A: It has certainly prepared me for the long hours! (although I now work hard mentally, compared to physically behind a bar). It has also taught me how to deal with people and given me confidence that I am making the right spirit for the right people at the right time.

Q: What advice would you give to bartenders who might try to get into similar businesses as yours?

A: Make sure you are 100% confident in your product and make sure you have worked through the business plan in detail before you launch onto the market.

> **gaz sez:** *This guy came a very long way in a relatively short time—hell, he's still in his mid-thirties! Most of you guys reading this might think that mid-thirties is on the old side, but believe me when I tell you that very few people accomplish what Alex has accomplished by his age.*
>
> *I guess my favorite line from Alex's Q & A is the one where he credits his time behind the bar for having taught him how to deal with people. We all know that that's true, and I don't think it can ever be stressed too much.*
>
> *Well done, Alex, you're a Fabulous Entrepreneur.*

SUNTORY
THE ART OF JAPANESE WHISKY
SINCE 1923

YAMAZAKI   HAKUSHU   HIBIKI

www.suntory.com/whisky
www.facebook.com/SuntoryWhisky

Yamazaki® and Hakushu® Single Malt Whiskies. Hibiki® Blended Whisky, each 43% alc./vol. (86 proof).
©2012 Imported by Suntory International Corp, New York, NY. Distributed by Skyy Spirits, LLC, San Francisco, CA.

PLEASE ENJOY RESPONSIBLY.

Alex Kratena

Artesian Bar at The Langham Hotel, London, England

gaz sez: *I don't know Alex really well, but our paths have crossed on a few occasions, most notably, for me at least, in 2010 when he and Francesco Orefici, the Bar Manager at Artesian, competed in a punch competition held by Courvoisier cognac in London. I was one of the judges that day, and the presentation that Alex and Francesco made literally brought tears to my eyes. Why? Because they get it.*

What do they get? As I've said time and time again, a bartender must wear many hats, and being of service to guests must always come first and foremost. When you enter a competition such as this one, though, all of your energy must go into the performance you put on. Oh, sure, the drink matters, too, and these guys went wild with their punch that day, but the prime focus was on performance, and Alex and Francesco did not disappoint.

There were quite a few good performances that day, so winning this competition wasn't an easy thing to do, but I think all of the other competitors will forgive me for saying that the guys from the Artesian put on an act worthy of Broadway.

Enough from me, let's let Alex take over for a while:

Q: How long have you worked behind the bar?

A: I've been working behind bars since I was legally entitled to do so.

Q: What do you love, and what do you hate, about bartending?

A: I love the beginning of each night, the smell of perfume, tension, and lights down, music, atmosphere and the expectations of what the night will bring us. I hate broken glass washers, barbacks calling in sick, running out of goods, the ice machine not functioning properly and falling asleep on computer when trying to put the orders through 4 am in the morning.

Q: What advice would you give to people who want to become bartenders?

A: Work hard and always do your very best, always go the extra mile, always do more than others, always do different things than others, be more committed than others, sleep less than others. You will manage more. The world belongs to those who see its full potential!

Q: In what direction do you see the craft going in the next 5 years?

A: Together we will make this industry better, that will bring us more guests and we will all do more and better!

Q: Anything else you'd like to add?

A: Pop in for drink whenever you are in London!

gaz sez: Inviting me for a drink went a long way toward enamoring me of Alex! Seriously, though: I love the advice he gives here about going the extra mile. From time to time I hear people saying, "how come this bartender or that bartender gets all the attention in the press?" There's an answer to that. They are the people who go the extra mile. Thanks, Alex, you're a Fabulous Bartender.

Cheryl Charming

Bombay Club, New Orleans LA, USA

gaz sez: *It's hard for me to remember when I first "met" Cheryl Charming, though I know that she and I corresponded for a long time via email before we were finally face to face at Tales of the Cocktail in New Orleans. And Cheryl lived up to her reputation as a wildly creative bartender, and a unique character to boot, from the moment I met her.*

Cheryl is one of those bartenders who just won't quit. She seems to have her fingers in so many pies at any given moment in time, and she always manages to juggle all of her projects without ever letting a single ball drop. To say that she's a Fabulous Bartender is an understatement at best.

Before I hand you over to Cheryl's questionnaire answers, I'm going to list some of her accomplishments so you can try to digest the enormity of her feats over the years.

Cheryl Charming has 14 books to her name, she makes customized résumés and business cards for bartenders, she's a graphic designer and she's a magician who has created her own line of cocktail-related jewelry that's available, with lots of other bar-related goodies, at Ms. Charming's on-line Bar Store, and she also created Ms. Charming's Drink Trivia App. That's the tip of the iceberg, I think. Over to Cheryl.

Q: How long have you worked behind the bar?

A: Since 1980.

Q: Name the bars where you worked, and what cities they are in.

A: I've worked all over America, but the bulk of my experience was with Walt Disney World in Orlando, FL and Commodore Cruise Lines in Miami.

Q: What do you love, and what do you hate, about bartending?

A: Initially, I loved the money. Through the years I learned to love the people and connections made. I don't hate anything.

Q: What advice would you give to people who want to become bartenders?

A: Wow, I have books and a website that offer pages of information, but if I had to put it in a nutshell I'd say get behind a bar, become a sponge, ask questions, read books, and learn everything you can from the best people in the business.

Q: In what direction do you see the craft going in the next 5 years?

A: This is something that is challenging to predict. I believe the combination of media exposure (film, music, TV, etc) combined with the introduction of new products always shapes the craft. Especially, on the mass level.

Q: Anything else you'd like to add?

A: There are many things, but the one at the top of the list is appreciation. Bartending is very physical with cleaning, stocking, hauling trash, etc. Each time I've had to haul out the trash, inside I am appreciating the trash because it's proof that I had a busy night, which gave me money to pay my bills and use for pleasure. I've learned that a state of appreciation in all I do only manifests more good in my life.

> **gaz sez:** *THERE'S MUCH WISDOM IN THIS SENTENCE:*
>
> *"Each time I've had to haul out the trash, inside I am appreciating the trash because it's proof that I had a busy night, which gave me money to pay my bills and use for pleasure."*
>
> *Lots of us can learn from that one, so you might want to think about it. I certainly did.*

Christopher "Hal" Halleron

Hoboken NJ, USA

gaz sez: *I think I first met Hal in 2003 when he attended Cocktails in the Country, the bartender workshop I used to hold at Painter's Tavern, my local joint in Cornwall-on-Hudson, NY. He and I just seemed to hit it off straight away, and that's why I got back in touch with him the following year to ask him to come take the workshop again.*

What had happened, you see, is that I was diagnosed with tongue cancer in late 2003, and although I'd had what turned out to be a very successful operation to take care of the matter, at that point I wasn't quite sure how much longer I had to live. They give you a 50/50 chance of living for 5 years if you get tongue cancer, and mine had been stage two.

With that in mind, the reason I asked Hal to come take the workshop for a second time was that I figured that he was exactly the right man to take over from me should ill health prevent me from holding more Cocktails in the Country sessions. I couldn't think of anyone better suited for the job. Hal had all the right values, and he's as down-to-earth as a man can be.

I never really asked Hal whether or not he wanted to take the job should I fall ill again, I just explained the situation and he dutifully came up to the Hudson Valley and took the course again. I should probably mention that we had a really good time that weekend!

Hal doesn't tend bar these days, but he has the soul of a bartender, and in my eyes, no matter what he does for a living (he's a freelance writer at present), Christopher "Hal" Halleron will always be a bartender. As I said in the intro to this chapter, it's the highest compliment I can think of. Over to Hal, now.

Q: How long have you worked behind the bar?

A: Twelve years.

Q: Name the bars where you worked, and what cities they are in.

A: Duffy's—Hoboken, New Jersey

Q: What do you love, and what do you hate, about bartending?

A: I love(d) the respect, when I get (got) it. It comes few and far between, but among the endlessly churning sea of oblivious ingrates and boorish belligerents, there is the odd customer that can see a bartender who is trying to elevate the craft—not only the craft of making drinks but also serving them, thereby making people stay or at least come back for another one.

I hate(d) the disrespect—which comes in so many forms. And I hate New Year's Eve… Any bartender who claims to enjoy working New Year's Eve is either a neophyte or a masochist.

Q: What advice would you give to people who want to become bartenders?

A: Be pragmatic. This is NOT a hobby, whether you do it five nights a week or five hours a month, this is work—hard work. Know your strengths, shore up your weaknesses and take nothing too personally.

Pick your battles. It's the one service job where the customer is not always right, but that doesn't mean you always have to be an asshole about it. Just give what you get and you'll feel good about what you do.

Q: In what direction do you see the craft going in the next 5 years?

A: Frankly, I see it going downhill on the whole. Customer service is eroding across the board, and therefore the bar (no pun intended) is set pretty low. With the notable exception of a few anachronistic bastions of integrity, most bar owners look at the bottom line—so the market favors the lower skill set, and anyone who has done it long enough to know what the hell they are doing has already banged their head on the income ceiling. By and large it's a transient trade with a short shelf life... like pro athletes, but with no pension.

Q: Anything else you'd like to add?

A: Like anything in life, bartending is what you make of it. I'm fiercely proud of my years standing behind the bar. It has had a profound effect on who I am and will undoubtedly shape the man I become long after I've hung up the apron. On the whole, bartenders are the most empathetic people I have ever known—which is the best characteristic you could ask for in a human being.

Cris Dehlavi

M Restaurant, Columbus OH, USA

gaz sez: *I first met Cris Dehlavi on-line when she submitted a recipe for consideration in the 2011 batch of 101 Best New Cocktails. Her drink, Marquee, made it through to the finals and it was included in last year's Annual Manual for Bartenders.*

Cris and I then exchanged a few emails, and we finally met at Tales of the Cocktail last July. She was an apprentice (it was the second year that she had toiled for the good of other bartenders there), and she was in the room when I gave a short talk to a bunch of similar-minded young souls. Then we met on stage at the annual Awards Show at Tales, but we never did have an actual conversation.

Why, then, did I select Cris Dehlavi to be a recipient of a Fabulous Bartender Award this year? Because, according to more than a few very trusted sources, it was Cris who single-handedly got the cocktail scene in Columbus off the ground. And that takes some doing.

I'm quite sure that Cris herself would never make that claim, and I'm also pretty certain that there have been lots of other bartenders in Columbus who have helped get the bartender scene going there, but Cris has been at the helm of the movement according to everyone I've spoken to about her accomplishments.

Well done, Cris. You're most certainly a Fabulous Bartender. Now let's hear what Cris has to say for herself.

Q: How long have you worked behind the bar?

A: I have been in the restaurant business since I was a child when my father owned one. I have been bartending for about 15 years.

Q: Name the bars where you worked, and what cities they are in.

A: I grew up in Tucson, Arizona; and worked in a number of restaurants around the city. The last 9 ½ years I have worked at M Restaurant in Columbus, Ohio, as the head bartender.

Q: What do you love, and what do you hate, about bartending?

A: I love the social aspect of bartending—my regulars are like extended family. I love meeting new people and having the ability to create cocktails for them. The craft is something I embrace every day. What do I hate ? The only thing I dislike is the long, late hours—but it's part of the deal and the good outweighs the bad every time.

Q: What advice would you give to people who want to become bartenders?

A: My advice would be to really study and learn as much as you can—read books, go to seminars. BarSmarts is a fantastic program I encourage all bartenders to go through. And be creative—there are no rules in what we do.

Q: In what direction do you see the craft going in the next 5 years?

A: I see the craft continuing to showcase fresh ingredients—building on the classics but also having the creativity to develop new ideas. I think we will continue to see new high quality spirits come on the market as well.

Q: Anything else you'd like to add?

A: This community of bartenders/mixologists around the US and really the world grows every day and yet we are a tight knit group….you really feel that when you go to events like Tales of the Cocktail where you are in a room with hundreds of people and yet everyone knows everyone!! Very cool! I wouldn't be where I am today if it wasn't for the incredible opportunity I had to work side by side with the greatest people in our industry.

The only other thing I'd like to add is just how important hospitality is to me—we are all so caught up in the craft but I think making the personal impact on every single person at the bar is worth its weight in gold.

> **gaz sez:** *Dwell on that last paragraph if you will. The sentiment behind it is also worth its weight in gold.*

Dushan Zaric

Employees Only & countless other ventures, New York NY, USA

gaz sez: *Dushan is one of my brothers from another mother. It's fairly amazing how we almost look like twins, though, huh? Our accents are pretty similar, too, I think. Okay, maybe not. I didn't know Dushan very well at all when I attended a cocktail competition at Employees Only a couple of years ago, and I mentioned to him that I was thinking of holding some Mindful Bartending workshops. His little eyes lit up. He told me that he and Aisha Sharpe had been holding very similar workshops for a while at that point. I think that that night cemented our bond.*

If you spend any time at all with Dushan Zaric, you're bound to see an impish smile leap to his face at some point, and when you see that smile you'll be reminded of an eight-year-old kid who just got an ice-cream, a bicycle, and a puppy all at once. The man is at once a wise old sage and an innocent child. Did I mention he fixes a decent drink, too?

This year I'm giving Dushan a nod, not only because of his wisdom, his generosity, and his cocktailian skills. I'm saluting the man because he's also an incredible entrepreneur. Here's what he has to say for himself.

We'll get the ball rolling with a list of businesses that Dushan is involved in:

Employees Only, 510 Hudson, New York NY 10014

Macao Trading Co, 311 Church Street, New York NY 10013

EO Brands, 510 Hudson, New York NY 10014

The 86 Spirits Co, 154 Grand Street, New York NY 10013

Bar Solution, 528 Carlton Ave, #1, Brooklyn NY 11238

Sarva Yoga Academy, 61 4th Ave, #3, New York NY 10003

Q: How long did you work behind the bar?

A: Sixteen years.

Q: Name the bars where you worked, and what cities they are in.

A: Street Pub, Santorini, Greece; Lush Club, Ios, Greece; Network Café, Queens, NY; Les Halles, NYC; Lot 61, NYC; Pravda, NYC; Balthazaar, NYC; Pastis, NYC; Schillers, NYC; Employees Only, NYC; Macao Trading Co, NYC.

Q: What did you love, and what did you hate, about bartending?

A: I love the ongoing opportunity to be of service and to inspire my apprentices. That keeps me on my toes and prevents me to obsess constantly about myself, which is so rejuvenating. The creative aspect of bartending is certainly a big part of my devotion to the craft and has been the emotional anchor and outlet for me in the years past.

I don't really have any pet peeves with the craft, maybe only dishonest, self-important and angry bartenders.

Q: How did you start up your present business or businesses?

A: I partnered up with fellow bartenders from Pravda in 2003 and we decided to open up a restaurant with a strong beverage & cocktail program as we felt that the time was right for us to venture into ownership. Little did we know that we would be one of the pioneers of the resurgence of the cocktail and inspire so many other bartenders and industry people to become entrepreneurs themselves. We also wanted to work on the premises ourselves as much as possible either behind the bar on the floor as managers in order to be closer to our guests and really make them feel welcome in our home. Through that we achieved a special atmosphere and environment of hospitality that was sincere and genuine.

The rest of the businesses were just a consequence of the success we had with EO. Macao Trading Co was a natural evolution for us as we wanted to emphasize the restaurant aspect of our gastronomical philosophy. Its unique concept allowed our creativity both in concept design as in operations to really mature.

EO Brands came from the decision to mass produce and bottle our home-made ingredients we successfully used in our cocktail programs. The idea is to produce and market all-natural, mostly non-alcoholic, craft bar mixers and cordials and help the home enthusiasts and other restaurants to elevate the level of their cocktails.

So far we have launched the following flavors: EO Grenadine, EO Lime Cordial, EO Bloody Mary Mix, EO Clover Honey Syrup, EO Letherwood Honey Syrup, EO Orange Agave Nectar, EO Sangrita (for Blanco Tequilas), EO Spicy Mango Sangrita (for Reposado Tequilas) and EO Spicy Chocolate Mole (for Añejo Tequilas).

The 86 Spirits company is my own partnership with a few other kindred spirits in order to source out and launch a "premium well" line of 5 distilled spirits, traditionally used in the speed rack or "well" behind most bars. The spirits chosen are of a very high quality with a specific ability to be highly mixable. We hope to launch a vodka, London Dry Gin, 100% Blue Agave Tequila, 3 year Blanco Rum and a Rye Whiskey in 2012.

Bar Solution is my restaurant consulting and training company.

Sarva Yoga Academy is a partnership with a friend and fellow teacher Michael Hewett. We offer a 7-month introduction course into philosophy of Yoga, Tibetan Buddhism and Gurdjieff's Fourth Way teaching.

Q: Do you think that being a bartender helped to prepare you for the work you do now?

A: Working behind the bar, working with people and serving both guests and fellow employees has taught me a great deal about myself and others. It has also shown me which skills to hone and what to watch out for. It has put me in contact with most amazing people from all walks of life including meeting all of my current investors and business partners in all my enterprises. So – for me bartending continues to serve as kind of a portal through which I meet people and inspire and teach young bartenders and apprentices.

Q: What advice would you give to bartenders who might try to get into similar businesses as yours?

A: Have a clear idea of what it is you want, inform yourself in as much detail as possible about what it is you are going for. Then devise a plan and in that plan include "unforeseen" events that are sure to come your way. Question every aspect of your concept with others, preferably with people you trust and look up to. Take their advice not as criticism but as help to get where you want. Arm yourself with patience and wisdom and above all be flexible. If you are going into partnership remember that in a proper functioning partnership every party works and contributes as much as they can for the good of the partnership. That means that you will be put into situations in which you'll learn to consider other people's opinions, their ideas and attitudes which would sometimes be directly opposite to yours. So – choose your partners wisely and then when you do make every effort to make it a success.

Q: Anything else you'd like to add?

A: Life has placed everyone on a path that is unique and special to that specific individual. It might be a smart idea therefore not to compare oneself with others. We are all very different and have different abilities and talents. In my world it has proven to be true that I receive exactly what I have deserved, both in positive and negative ways. So – if one wants anything—success in business, a career, a caring and loving emotional partner, etc…make sure that someone gets it first before you. For example, if you wish to own a profitable restaurant make sure that you make every effort to help your current employer be as successful and as profitable as possible. If you want a girlfriend or boyfriend then help others be less lonely, like befriending an elderly person in a retirement home and visiting them every week or so…etc, etc…

It is in your best self-interest not to think about your self-interest.

> **gaz sez:** *I learn so much at the feet of Dushan, and if you read what he wrote above, I'll wager that you, too, will benefit from his wisdom. Thanks Dushan.*

Joaquin Simo

Death & Co, New York NY, USA

gaz sez: *Joaquin is one of those bartenders who tends toward going about his business in a very quiet way, never hogging the limelight, never craving to be the center of attention. But he's always there. Always.*

Joaquin Simo crops up all over the damned place, and it was my good fortune to bump into him at an airport—God only knows which one—when we were both flying home from some boozy event or other. We managed to change our seats so we could chat on the plane, and his quiet yet confident demeanor shone right through.

Joaquin is what I might call one of the most solid citizens of today's bartending community, and you'll understand why the man's been successful in his career if you read his answers in the following questionnaire.

MOST IMPORTANTLY, I think, take a look at the advice he offers to people who are considering becoming bartenders. There's many a pearl of wisdom in that answer—you might want to think about sharing it with anyone who mentions that they are thinking of becoming a bartender.

Joaquin Simo, you're a very Fabulous Bartender, and I'm proud to be able to call you a friend. Over to you:

Q: How long have you worked behind the bar?

A: Ten years.

Q: Name the bars where you worked, and what cities they are in.

A: Death & Co, NYC; Stanton Social, NYC; Camino Sur, NYC; NoHo Star, NYC; Great Scott, Boston; White Horse Tavern, Boston.

Q: What do you love, and what do you hate, about bartending?

A: I love being the recipient of trust. My customers trust that I can and will read their moods, present company and specific situation, and base their service accordingly. A first (or third) date requires a very different style of service than bringing in a boss (or underlings or old college buddies) and I relish the chance to correctly interpret what someone needs (or doesn't need) from me and delivering each time. What do I hate? The lack of health care/insurance, paid vacations, and retirement benefits that typify the overwhelming majority of jobs in our industry.

Q: What advice would you give to people who want to become bartenders?

A: Ask yourself why you want to do it and base your bar career accordingly. First of all, start of by barbacking or bussing. If you can't handle the rigors of being support staff, then you have no business being a server. Barbacking may not be glamorous but it teaches you invaluable lessons about pacing, preparation, anticipation and teamwork.

These are the bedrock skills that every bartender should have aced before they're ever allowed to pour a shot or pull a pint for a guest.

If you're looking for a job with flexible hours that generally pays cash to help put yourself through school or to subsidize your true calling (painting, writing, dancing, day-trading, surfing, whatever) then go find an established high-volume spot with plenty of staff. If you want to make a career out of it, then work at as many different types of establishments as possible and make sure you learn useful lessons from each. Pick up speed & efficiency at a club, refine the art of making and maintaining regulars at a pub, learn about various beers, wines, spirits, foods and points of service at restaurants (from brewpubs to fine-dining) and lastly concentrate on learning and executing classic cocktails and creating original cocktails. There are too many inexperienced bartenders who get bit with the cocktail bug and allow their preoccupation with what's in the glass to supersede the needs of the guest who ordered it. Learning how to bartend has almost nothing to do with memorizing recipes or historical factoids. If your guests have no other reason than the quality of your drinks to return to your bar, then start learning how to talk to them about something other than bitters or bury yourself in service bar where there's no chance that you may have to interact with a paying customer.

Q: In what direction do you see the craft going in the next 5 years?

A: I see more restaurants taking their beverage programs more seriously—hopefully leading to a truer marriage between the front and back of the house. Hopefully, more "regular" bars will begin to turn away from prepackaged sour mixes and simply juice a la minute for their margaritas and sours, though that may never come true for the really high-volume spots. There's so much creativity that is yet to come and some truly innovative techniques/technology that are just emerging that could really push drinks in delicious new directions (see The Aviary and Booker & Dax). There's never been a better time to be a bartender, what with the plethora of information and tools readily available, but hopefully the true craft of bartending and hospitality is what is passed along, rather than simply the "art of mixology". Going from the one side of the bar to the other, then hopping to a brand ambassador position all within 2-3 year's time is simply not sustainable and does no one (especially the poor guests and bar managers who have to suffer these fools not so gladly) any favors.

Q: Anything else you'd like to add?

A: Treating our guests as such requires disabusing ourselves of the notion that being polite, courteous, & professional with guests is ever simply a "part" of our job as a server that we can elect not to do. Being exhausted, grumpy, pissy or distracted does not grant us license to forget that what we fundamentally do for a living is customer service and bartending/serving/hosting falls under that umbrella. Dropping menus, prepping garnishes, making cocktails and cleaning up our stations all fall under the umbrella of our jobs as servers (and don't think for a second any of those are optional either) but treating guests and coworkers with courtesy and respect is inescapable. Our jobs as a whole are simply one branch of customer service, and we must never lose sight of that.

Oh, and fer the love of gawd, don't shake my fuckin' Negroni.

Marian Beke

Nightjar, London, England

gaz sez: *I first met Marian in 2007 on the island of Bendor, just off the south coast of France. I was there with Mardee conducting a bartender workshop, hosted by Anistatia Miller and Jared Brown, my friends, and the publishers of this very book. Erik Lorincz was there, too, along with many other top-notch European bartenders. We had quite a blast.*

Marian's first job behind the bar was at Paparazzi, a fabulous joint in Bratislava, Slovakia (I tended bar there myself for a few hours in November, 2007). It's the place where Stan Vadrna trained lots and lots of Slovaks on the craft of the bartender, and Stan's tutelage had far-reaching effects. Go to any big city today—Paris, Sydney, San Francisco, New York, London—and if you visit the top cocktail bars there, you're almost certain to find a Slovak behind the stick of more than a couple of them.

Over a year after I met Marian in Bendor, I was asked to put on some sort of presentation at the Merchant Hotel in Belfast. Sean Muldoon had been nagging me for months to do this, and since David Wondrich was going to be there, too, I figured I should go and see if I could persuade him to buy me a drink. It didn't happen.

What did happen, though, was that Marian flew in from London and helped out behind the bar that weekend, just to be a part of the experience. That told me a lot about Marian. He's a bartender with passion. Marian, you're a Fabulous Bartender. Let's hear what he has to say for himself, huh?

Q: How long have you worked behind the bar?

A: For 9 years now.

Q: Name the bars where you worked, and what cities they are in.

A: Paparazzi, Bratislava; Townhouse, London; Montgomery Place, London; Artesian Bar, Langham Hotel, London; Purl, London; Nightjar, London.

Q: What do you love, and what do you hate, about bartending?

A: I love the fact that every day is different, [and] creating unique and extraordinary experiences with every guest for one moment only, which can be reappeared in similar way but never same again.

Also trying to create drinks as [an] experience rather than serving beverage make me feel happy.

I don't hate anything in my job [but] there are few things I might not like as much ([such as] drunk and rude people) but that's a small part of it.

Q: What advice would you give to people who want to become bartenders?

To ask themselves Why ? As many bartenders cannot answer this question then you can see people who are unhappy behind the bar or taking their job as a quick money maker. It is a profession as any other plus it requires really hard work and creativity to become good.

Q: In what direction do you see the craft going in the next 5 years?

A: I'm not a witch who can read out of magic cards but wish to see it continue in similar way as it is now. The whole world is shaking for better service and drinks, people getting trained and being interested in being a good bartender rather than waiting 3 months then jumping away to do an ambassador job etc.

Q: Anything else you'd like to add?

A: Just to say big thank you to our guests (and you Gary!) as they are the holy grail of all bars and sometimes we as a bartenders forget that.

Monica Berg
Aqua Vitae, Oslo, Norway

gaz sez: *First I heard from Monica Berg was by way of a cocktail recipe she submitted for consideration as one of this year's 101 Best New Cocktails, and the drink, What is Hip, was truly spectacular. It made it into the book. Next thing I knew of this woman was when I met her in France last year. Monica was a finalist in the G'Vine Gin Connoisseurs competition, an annual event at which I've been a judge since its inception in 2010. It's something I always look forward to—a week in Cognac hanging with Philip Duff, Audrey Fort, Jean-Sebastien Robiquet, and various and sundry top-notch bartenders from around the globe. What could be bad?*

I loved spending time with Monica in France, getting to know her bartending philosophies and cocktailian skills, and I loved practicing drunken yoga with her on the balcony of the farmhouse where the closing night part was held. My Downward Dog has never been so inspired before.

These events spurred me to pick Monica as one of this year's Fabulous Bartenders, then, and what sealed the deal was the fact that this woman shows up absolutely everywhere. I went to Germany for the Bar Convent, and there was Monica. She was in London for their Cocktail Week, too. *Monica is a go-getter, and she knows how to pull it off. Monica is a Fabulous Bartender. Over to Ms. Berg.*

Q: How long have you worked behind the bar?

A: I guess it's been about 10 years now, (times sure flies when you're having fun!)

Q: Name the bars where you worked, and what cities they are in.

A: SOM, Cheval and ICEBAR by ICEHOTEL All of them are in Oslo.

(I also had a rather fun summer working in a couple of bars in Crete when I was 19 just passing time until I turned 20 and could legally work in bars in Norway.)

Q: What do you love, and what do you hate, about bartending?

A: I think what I love most is the "rush" of happiness you get when you manage to match the perfect drink with the perfect guest, seeing how their face lights up and knowing that you contributed to that.

I don't think I hate anything about being a bartender but of course some things are more boring than others. If I had to pinpoint something, I'd say the only thing I (might) hate about being a bartender is the misconception people have about what it actually means being a bartender by choice and not just passing time before finding a "real" job.

PART 2 • THE MINDFUL BARTENDER

Q: What advice would you give to people who want to become bartenders?

A: My philosophy has always been to work hard, be patient and challenge yourself as often as you can. The only way to improve is by practicing, it might take a while but that only makes it so much better when you finally master it. Everything is new the first time you try it – and it's like that for everyone.

Q: In what direction do you see the craft going in the next 5 years?

A: I think bars and bartenders will embrace diversity even more and keep pushing the boundaries of what is considered to be a "normal" cocktail bar. I really love the fact that bartenders are quite curious and experimental by nature, and there is a kind of "sky's the limit/nothing goes untested" attitude towards basically everything. I think we'll keep seeing things be taken to the extreme – be it extreme attention to details when it comes to classics, or extreme as in pushing new techniques.

Q: Anything else you'd like to add?

A: I am truly amazed by all the great things I've gotten to experience thru working as a bartender, and not to forget all the amazing people I've met! In my mind this is the best industry in the world and I'm so grateful to be a part of it! Also —Gary, when are your world famous finger-stirred Negronis coming to Oslo?

Murray Stenson

Canon, Seattle, WA, USA

gaz sez: *I first met Murray in 1995 or 1996 when Mardee and I were on a book tour with our* Book of Bourbon. *We did a signing in Seattle and Murray showed up. He was one of the most enthusiastic bartenders I'd ever met.*

Known as The Flash, obviously because of his speed and accuracy behind the bar, Murray is much loved by his regulars, and all who encounter the man are instantly impressed by his warmth and knowledge, but there's something else about Murray that makes him stand head and shoulders above most other bartenders, and in order to let you in on this, I'm turning you over now to Nidal Ramini, the London bartender/bar owner who was, in large part, responsible for joints such as Dusk and Montgomery Place.

About 5 or 6 years ago (2006 would be guess), I was looking for a copy of **The Fine Art of Mixing Drinks** as a gift for Ago Perrone. Ago had been with me for 3 years at Dusk and he was just about to open Montgomery Place for me. It had been a long project, as crazy as it sounds now, the idea of prohibition style cocktails being available outside of hotel bars was not something that London (MnH aside) had embraced and therefore Ago and I had spent a lot of time researching recipes and concepts for the Montgomery list (FYI, the list today is pretty much identical to the one that you'll find in the bar today) so I wanted to give him something special as a "thank you" for all his work. I went onto Ebay and lo and behold I found not only a copy of TFAOMD but one signed by Embury himself and at a pretty reasonable price (sub $30 if memory serves). Anyway, I put a bid in and waited for the auction to end. About 5 mins before the end I got online and found that I'd been outbid, I then went through the usual bid tennis with the other party when my connection died. I got back online to find that I'd lost the book to a bid of around $80. I quickly emailed the winner saying that I'd be prepared to offer him a "double your money deal" on the book as it was a gift etc etc etc. I got another note back saying that unfortunately he too was planning to use the book as a gift, to a regular in his bar, an employee of Microsoft (he lived in Seattle) and a big cocktail fan.

Recognising a kindred spirit, we got chatting and it turned out that the winning bidder was one Murray Stenson of the Zig Zag café (I believe at the time they were championing the Last Word cocktail, so I knew a lot about the bar). We talked about the scene in London and Seattle and I told him all about Montgomery and what we were planning on doing. We exchanged emails for a few days and then he told me that he'd sent me a present in the post. The very next day I received a copy of TFAOMD, OK so it wasn't the signed version, but I believe it was a 1958 version and a book selling for between $70-$100 on Ebay. I was completely blown away by this and I remember posting something on Drink Boy about the fact that it goes to show what a great world we operate in, that two people, who had never met each other, had this infinity purely based on shared passions. Amazing!

Murray and I continued to stay in touch, he would always recommend customers of his to Montgomery when they were over in London and I was able to show them the book and share the story. You see, I never actually gave Ago the book, I told him the story and he was equally taken aback so when we commissioned a "trophy cabinet" for want of a better phrase, in Montgomery alongside things such as an original Trader Vic menu, some antique julep cups and cocktail tools we placed Murray's Embury book in there so we could show people the treasure gained from the joys of bartending.

I still actually tell that story and I'd be delighted if you could retell it at Tales. Also, I'm pretty sure that the recipient of book was Mr Robert Hess (cocktail lover, Microsoft employee?) so it would be good to hear if he still has the book.

–Nidal Ramini

gaz sez: *Quite a story, huh? Murray Stenson is a Fabulous Bartender. Let's hear what he has to say for himself.*

Q: How long have you worked behind the bar?

A: Since 1976—36 years.

Q: Name the bars where you worked, and what cities they are in.

A: Oliver's (in the Mayflower Park Hotel) in the 1970s; Daniel's Broiler and Leschi in the 1980s; Il Bistro, 1990s; Zig Zag Café, 2000s. All located in Seattle.

Q: What do you love, and what do you hate, about bartending?

A: I love meeting customers. What I hate about it is missing out on live music performances.

Q: What advice would you give to people who want to become bartenders?

A: I always tell the young ones you go into for three reasons: Sex, power and money.

> **gaz sez:** *that's my all-time fave answer to that question!*

Q: In what direction do you see the craft going in the next 5 years?

A: In the last 10 years it has gone from a niche market to the more mainstream. I see that growth continuing.

Q: Anything else you'd like to add?

A: It's been fun.

Paul "The Mixxa" Martin

Bartender, Trainer, & All-Around Good Guy, Brighton, England

gaz sez: *I first met Paul Martin in the late 1990s when Paul Pacult and I hosted a syndicated radio show call The Happy Hour. We were among the very first people in the USA to air ads for liquor, and since we were the only game in town, radio-wise, industry people jumped through hoops to be on the show. Paul Martin didn't need to jump through hoops, though. Within minutes of meeting the man it was obvious that he was one of the good guys.*

"How do you bill yourself," I asked him, on air.

"I think of myself as a Roaming Cocktail Warrior," he told us.

Need I say more?

According to his web site (cocktailentertainment.com), "Paul 'The Mixxa' Martin is an international award winning cocktail mixologist and twice holder of the Guinness World Record for the 1-hour cocktail speed mix. Paul is the author of the globally successful World Encyclopaedia of Cocktails and Mammoth Book of Cocktails as well as being the presenter of numerous cocktail mixing DVD's. He has appeared on more than 40 TV shows demonstrating his cocktail skills and has travelled extensively to entertain audiences from New York to Moscow . . . Paul also has a reputation as one of the drinks industry's most inspirational trainers. He has created and delivered national training courses for many top brands including TGI Fridays, Pitcher & Piano & All Bar One. With more than 15 years of live performance experience, Paul's unique combination of entertainment skills and world-class mixology has resulted in him hosting the ultimate in interactive corporate entertainment and team building shows."

None of the accomplishments mentioned above figured into me hailing Paul as a Bartender's Bartender this year, though. What clinched it for me was the fact that he started filming instructional cocktail videos, complete with sign language. I've seen a lot of innovation within our industry over the past few years, and this was one of the very best. Well done, my friend. You are, indeed, a Fabulous Bartender.

Let's hear what Paul has to say for himself:

Q: How long have you worked behind the bar?

A: In one form or another, it's been more than quarter of a century (27 years to be precise), although for the last 15 years my work has been mainly on 'this' side of the bar.

Q: Name the bars where you worked, and what cities they are in.

A: The most memorable bars were Coconut Grove, Peppermint Park, Maxwells, Chicago Rib Shack, Henry J Beans,

[G'VINE®] GINS DE FRANCE

01 TX

So traditionally Unconventional www.g-vine.com

LS Grunts, all of which were in London, Pickwick's in Hampton Court, and my own bar, Kudos, in Brighton.

Q: What do you love, and what do you hate, about bartending?

A: I love the international language of bartending. It transcends geographical and cultural (most of them) boundaries. Hate is a strong word, but.... I have never liked the arrogance and ignorance that rears its head too often in our industry. I have spent much of the last 15 years helping to eradicate these attitudes from our bartenders. There is absolutely no place for it with the modern mixologist.

Q: What advice would you give to people who want to become bartenders?

A: It's a career choice that has more potential for success, creativity and job satisfaction than in any previous era. If people are serious about a bartending career, there couldn't be a better time to start. However, I would suggest that without a true passion for the role, it may be difficult to succeed.

Q: In what direction do you see the craft going in the next 5 years?

A: The future for the development of our industry lies in an improved ability to communicate effectively. Bar skills are a fundamental requirement but alone they are simply not enough. Great drinks need to be presented and delivered by excellent communicators for the 'craft' to evolve in the interest of the guest/customer. Otherwise, it all becomes a bit self-serving and incestuous!

Phoebe Esmon

The Farmer's Cabinet, Philadelphia PA, USA

gaz sez: *I met Phoebe a few years ago when I was helping Pernod-Ricard USA at some events in Philadelphia, and apart from being admittedly gob-smacked by her stunning appearance and demeanor, I was also struck by just how seriously she took her job. Couple that with a light-hearted personality, a sense of style that makes her stand out from the rest, and a boyfriend, Christian Raphael Gaal, who works with her at The Farmer's Market and has just as much style and charisma as Phoebe, an you have the makings of a Fabulous Bartender.*

Here's what Phoebe has to say for herself:

Q: How long have you worked behind the bar?

A: Seven years.

Q: Name the bars where you worked, and what cities they are in.

A: Some when I was in college, then there was a window when I was away from the industry, but was spending a lot of time doing research and reading about cocktail phenomena and movements. I don't really feel like I really started taking the job as seriously until I hit Philly. In Philly I have worked at The Ugly American, Chick's (Now renamed Chick's Social), Kennett So. 2nd (Christian and I did the program there together), Catahoula, Noble American Cookery, The Farmer's Cabinet (where I am at the moment).

Q: What do you love, and what do you hate, about bartending?

A: I love the way people who might never have spoken end up having great conversations, the comradeship created by an atmosphere of openness and hospitality, the way some people will stay away for months at a time, but always come back to sit with you again: to trade stories or be comforted or just to say "hi, I was thinking of you."

I hate it when something causes that special atmosphere to dissipate or to disappear. Drink-slinging/being a shaker-monkey, whatever you want to call it: the feeling of being a zoo exhibit is not a pleasant sensation.

Q: What advice would you give to people who want to become bartenders?

A: It's a lot harder than you think. A good bartender cares about the needs strangers. If you're only in it for the money, you might want to do something else. More than anything, bartending is a craft: like any other craft, be that plumbing or bookbinding, it requires skill acquired through study, practice and hard work. And patience. Lots and lots of patience.

Q: In what direction do you see the craft going in the next 5 years?

A: I expect that the speak-easy thing is going to go the way of the Dodo. I think craft cocktail bartending is going to be absorbed into a well-rounded bar program, where you will meet bartenders who can answer your questions about wine and beer just as easily as they can whip up the newest Manhattan variant from New York. Essentially, the return of the "Good Bar", and the death of the theme park bar.

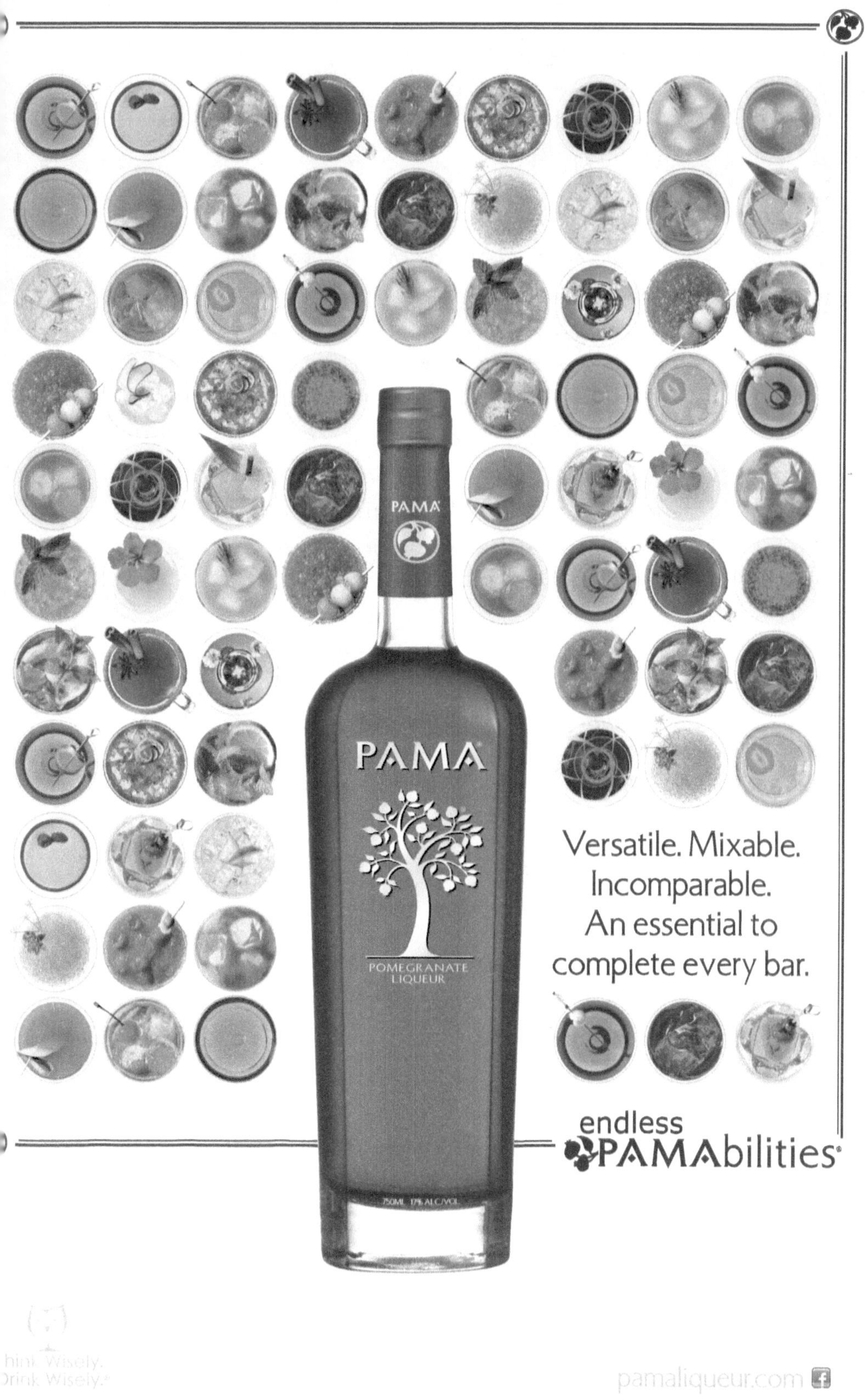
PAMA
PAMA
POMEGRANATE LIQUEUR
Versatile. Mixable.
Incomparable.
An essential to
complete every bar.
endless
PAMAbilities
Think Wisely.
Drink Wisely.
pamaliqueur.com

Sasha Petraske

New York NY, USA

gaz sez: *I've always gotten along well with Sasha Petraske, and even though we haven't spent a massive amount of time together, we've bumped into each other at all sorts of events, and we flew across the Atlantic together back in 2008 (I think) when we were both headed to the London Bar Show. I've never thought of Sasha as being a bartender, though. I've always thought of him as being an entrepreneur, a businessman, and an innovator, but never as a bartender.*

Recently though, I read an interview with Sasha, and I'm damned if I can find it now, but within that article Sasha said something about the role of the bartender that knocked my socks off. Damn! I said to myself. This guy does have the soul of a bartender after all. (It was similar to Sasha's answer in the questionnaire below about what he loves about bartending.)

I'm fond of fessing up when I'm wrong about something, so I'm taking this opportunity to apologize to Sasha, and at the same time I'm bringing you his answers to my questionnaire. The will, I'm quite sure, serve to back up what I now know to be true. Sasha Petraski is a Fabulous Bartender.

PART 2 • THE MINDFUL BARTENDER

Q: How long have you been in the bar business?

A: I started bartending at a beer and wine only bar in '97, and opened Milk and Honey in 2000.

Q: Name the bars where you worked, and what cities they are in.

A: Von, NYC; Milk and Honey, NYC; Milk and Honey, London.

Q: What do you love, and what do you hate, about bartending?

A: [I love having] the opportunity to attempt to put one's ego aside for 9 hours, to try to be of service to people that you don't know.

I hate having to occasionally see people at their worst.

Q: What advice would you give to people who want to become bartenders?

A: Stop and think about whether you would rather be a famous artist, actor or musician, but at the same pay as a bartender. If the answer is "yes", do not go into service.

Q: In what direction do you see the craft going in the next 5 years?

A: I would like to think it will go in the direction of simplicity and humility, seen as a craft rather than an art.

I'm afraid that it is likely to go in the opposite direction, especially if there is a technological game-changer that makes it possible to create cellar temperature cocktails that can compare with a glass of fine wine or spirit.

WITH ARTISTRY COMES ACCOLADES.

Chinaco Reposado
BEST OF SHOW. BEST OF CATEGORY. GOLD MEDAL.
Spirits of Mexico Tasting Competition 2010

Chinaco Tequila, the only tequila made in the state of Tamaulipas, is aged for a minimum of eleven months in white oak barrels, and double distilled to achieve an exceptionally smooth and legendary flavor.

Luxardo Maraschino
GOLD MEDAL.
St. Louis World's Fair 1904

Still produced according to the original formula created in 1821, Luxardo Maraschino is distilled from homegrown Marasca cherries and carefully aged in special vats of Finnish ash wood. To date, it has won 56 Gold Medals.

Junípero Gin
DOUBLE GOLD.
San Francisco World Spirits Competition 2004

Junípero Gin is made by hand in the classic 'distilled dry gin' tradition, utilizing more than a dozen botanicals in their natural state, in a small copper pot still at the Anchor distillery.

The King's Ginger Liqueur
GOLD MEDAL. 91 POINTS. EXCEPTIONAL.
Beverage Testing Institute 2011

The King's Ginger is the emphatically ginger liqueur that was specifically formulated by Berry Bros. & Rudd in 1903 for King Edward VII. Rich and zesty, it was created to stimulate and revivify His Majesty, and has been appreciated by bon viveurs, sporting gentlemen and high-spirited ladies ever since.

Ypióca Ouro Cachaca
GOLD MEDAL. BEST CACHACA.
WSWA Tasting Competition 2011

Established in 1846, Ypióca's time honored method — and use of balsam wood barrels — has culminated in a selection of Cachaca showing unmistakable flavor and distinction as a fine spirit.

Hirsch Straight Bourbon Small Batch Reserve
GOLD MEDAL. BEST BOURBON.
WSWA Tasting Competition 2011

This hand-picked bourbon is distilled and aged in the Commonwealth of Kentucky. Hirsch Straight Bourbon Small Batch Reserve is selected for connoisseurs of small batch fine spirits.

PROVIDING THE BRIDGE BETWEEN DISCERNING BUYERS AND THE WORLD'S FINEST SPIRITS

ANCHOR DISTILLING COMPANY
SAN FRANCISCO
www.ANCHORDISTILLING.com

Q: Anything else you'd like to add?

A: Cocktails are not for thinking or opining about, but for experiencing.

Steve McDermott

The Bowery, Brisbane, Australia

gaz sez: *I'm not sure what year it was, though I'm tempted to say that it was around 2007, when I first set foot into Salvatore at Fifty, the fabulous private club that Salvatore Calabrese, the Maestro himself, made famous. I've told the story of how impressed I was with the service at that bar over and over again, and I've always given credit to Salvatore from training his staff so well. That credit still holds true, and there's someone else who deserves credit, too.*

Steve McDermott was behind the bar that night, and it was he who quickly figured out how I like to be treated at a bar. I like a bit of banter. Some back and forth. And if the bartender starts to take the piss out of me in a good-hearted manner, then I know that I've found another home away from home. And that's what Steve McDermott did for me that night. He made me feel at home.

Lest you're not aware of this, Salvatore at Fifty was a very posh joint. The kind of place in which you might expect the staff to yes-sir-no-sir-three-bags-full-sir you to death all night. And I'm quite sure that a lot of that went on in that bar, but Steve had been trained to trust his intuition, and he had learned to run with it. He figured me out pretty quickly, and I had one of the best nights I've ever had in a bar. Steve McDermott is a Fabulous Bartender. Here's what he has to say for himself.

Q: How long have you worked behind the bar?

A: Fourteen years.

Q: Name the bars where you worked, and the cities they are in.

A: Brasserie Bar at the Hyatt Regency, Coolum, Sunshine Coast; Black Dog Cafe, Mooloolaba, Sunshine Coast; The Light Bar, London; The Purple Bar, London; Salvatore at Fifty, London; Kanaloa, London; The Bowery, Brisbane.

Q: What do you love, and what do you hate, about bartending?

A: Love: Surpassing people's expectations, learning new things, teaching new things to others.

Hate: Bad manners, no matter which side of the bar it comes from.

Q: What advice would you give to people who want to become bartenders?

A: Know your job as best you can, pay close attention to the greats in our industry, work in the best bar you possibly can, smile!

Q: In what direction do you see the craft going in the next 5 years?

A: I would love to see brandies utilized more, in particular Cognac. I think the ever growing amount of small boutique cocktail bars will have a positive influence on service standards. I can definitely seethe trend towards food and cocktail pairinggaining momentum, I think a bar that can provide a highlevel of modern cuisine and cocktails will be the next big thing amongst consumers.

Q: Anything else you'd like to add?

A: A great big cheers to bartenders everywhere!

Tobin Ellis

Bar Magic, Las Vegas NV, USA

gaz sez: *If ever there was a bartender who knows what the job is all about it's Tobin Ellis, a guy who I've met just one time, unless I've met him a dozen times and don't remember—this tired old brain plays tricks sometimes. It was the luverly Charlotte Voissey of Hendrick's gin fame who introduced me to Tobin. The two of them had been helping a new joint, Shadows on the Hudson, get off the ground, and since I live pretty close to the place—it's about 60 miles north of Manhattan —Charlotte thought I might want to check it out. There was free booze involved. I went willingly.*

It was, indeed, a great night we had at Shadows, and I even went home relatively sober after turning down a chance to go bar hopping with a bunch of bartenders who were getting off work. It's seldom I turn down opportunities like this. I have no idea what got into me that night.

There was something about Tobin that turned me on. It was his passion. It was infectious. No wonder this guy trains bartenders, I thought. Who wouldn't want to be a bartender after listening to this guy's spiel for a while? He's a pretty special dude, is Tobin Ellis.

Since that time, Tobin and I have kept in touch

primarily on Facebook, though occasionally we exchange emails, too. And it was his thoughts on flair bartending that made me sit up and really pay attention to the man. He vocalized something I've believed for a long time. Flair is a very legitimate form of bartending. Here's what Tobin wrote:

Flair is nothing more than efficiency elevated to a higher physical level, with a healthy dose of passion thrown in. A tomahawk slam dunk is flair. Is there really any need to spin 360-degrees, stick your tongue out, spread your legs, palm the ball, pull it back, then slam the ball, and then pump your fists? No. But does it change the momentum of a game? Does it entertain? Does it inspire? Yes, yes, yes. Flair to me has always been more akin to the samurai then the circus clown. But I've always kind of lived out in the fringe.

Dushan [Zaric] has quite a lot of flair in his hands. Simon [Ford] is an admitted closet flair bartender. Gary your flair is your grace that defies logic—you seem to stumble and bobble about behind the wood and yet somehow your movements have a rhythm to them and though it appears you are just haphazardly tossing various ingredients together like some kind of Hogwarts wizard, you always end up putting a beautiful glass of yummy in front of people that is actually quite intelligent.

The cover of Dale's first book is the most common act of mixology flair: flaming the nearly invisible oils off the peel of a piece of fruit over a cocktail. A technique he championed and brought back from lord knows where or when. And Aisha [Sharpe]—as discussed today on Facebook, she's a Sith overlord, her flair is wicked.

I have sat back and 'quietly' watched for the past 10 to 11 years as slowly, the movements of flair have creeped into mixology—flair is everywhere now, nearly every heralded mixologist does more than they realize. And I can't even count how many mixologists have discreetly approached me, asking about the subject.

The notion that flair bartender is some young, cocky bartender 'juggling' bottles around is as much stereotyping as the mixologist [being] a stiff, stoic geek in a bowtie reciting obscure passages from a David Embury book while slowly making a rye cocktail with homemade bitters, boringly.

Sadly, examples of both of these dull creatures is alarmingly prevalent. In my mind, flair is simply a style of bartending, as is mixology. Both deserve respect and attention and then, once fairly well mastered or at least digested... they deserve forgetting, so the focus can return to the bar. The bar we tend. And the people on the other side of it.

I think the mixologists should spend less time fussing over their cocktails and the flair bartenders should spend less times trying to figure out how to balance a bottle on the back of their knee. Both should return to center, where all of you live."

gaz sez: *It's wisdom like this that makes Tobin Ellis a Fabulous Bartender. Good on you, Tobin. And before we let this matter drop, here's a word about Flair from KingCocktail himself:*

"Flair is a marriage of hospitality and theatre; and bartending has been that since the dawn of modern mixology in the early 19th century. Simon Diffford is hosting a flair conversation in Class *magazine and each time this conversation comes up, some in the cocktailian community showcontempt for what is different from them. We are all thrilled that bartending has embraced*

craft and real ingredients etc. but to my mind a cocktailian bartender who embraces elements of flair may be the perfect bartender."

—*Dale DeGroff, 2011*

Now let's hear what Tobin has to say for himself.

Q: Where were you born and raised?

A: Born: Los Gatos, California. Raised: West Irondequoit, New York (Rochester).

Q: How did you first get into the bar business?

A: I was 18 in college and landed a gig barbacking for the college graduation weekend. Shortly after I was also pouring beers at a popular college bar for my fraternity and at our house parties. I loved being behind the wood. Took a job as a dishwasher and waiter on campus and one day they needed someone to man a bar. I had a friend and bartender named Renee Rice show me how to cut fruit and how to pour a few recipes.

I bought a Mr. Boston's book and memorized as much as I could. A couple weeks later, I was asked to bartend at the president of the university's residence. His wife walked up to the bar and asked me if i knew how to make her favorite drink: a Pink Squirrel. I had memorized it because it was such a funny name. So even though we couldn't make it, I knew the recipe. She was impressed. I made her laugh and next thing I know I'm the personal bartender for all the events at the President's residence. It snowballed from there.

Q: Name the first 3 or more bars where you worked, please, and let us know what kind of bars they were.

A: 1. State University of Oswego College Catering Department: catering/banquets but I used fresh fruit to make whatever I could.

2. The Caddyshack: college "club" bar—high volume, cheap drinks.

3. The Shacki Patch, Oswego, NY: Small high-volume live music college bar for upperclassmen and locals.

4. TGI Friday's (Syracuse, Tyson's Corner VA) with a program that required memorization of 400 classic, fresh, and crazy recipes.

5. The Stoop, Syracuse, NY: Tequila and cocktail speakeasy opened in 1998. (Second floor spot with unmarked door, fresh program, classics, etc).

6. Sequoia, Georgetown, VA: High-volume, high-profile restaurant and outdoor bar next to the Kennedy Center. $100,000+ weekend nights.

7. Caesars Palace, Las Vegas: Head bartender and bar trainer. Later bartended at PURE Nightclub there as well.

Q: Who was your mentor?

A: Scott Mcintosh from TGI Friday's. He could do it all, seamlessly. This was back in the early '90s when believe it or not, TGI Friday's was one of the most-respected bar companies on the planet. He had the most knowledge, the most regulars, gave the highest level of service, made the best drinks, flipped bottles better than anyone, was funny, charming, fast, pulled great tips, always smiling and full of energy.

He did charity work for the community, trained all the service staff and just loved bartending. To this day I've never seen a bartender who was as "full package" of a bartender as Scottie. He's a conceirge now in one of the most famous yet under the radar 5-star hotels in Beverly Hills. He still bartends, just not with liquor bottles anymore.

Q: What came first: Flair, Mixology, or Being of service?

A: They are one. Truly, so all of them. The bartender's job is the selling, making, and serving quality profitable drinks in a warm, friendly and entertaining manner. Nobody ever used to compartmentalize bartending--- you had to do it all or you couldn't get a good job. Now everything is so specialized and frankly, lopsided with lots of gaping holes in people's skill sets.

Q: Was there a pivotal moment when your career went from good to "how the hell did I get here?"

A: When I took over The Stoop in the Armory Square of Syracuse, NY. I unknowingly created a speakeasy/cocktail program with a strong tequila and Margarita focus in 1998 that would go on to quickly become of the toast of the town. One week my work was featured on the front page of both local papers, on 2 of the 3 evening news channels, and a TV show on Food Network. We went from barely paying the bills to being packed almost every night of the week and won readers choice awards for "Best Margaritas" year after year. The offers came in after that including Tavern on the Green and Caesars Palace.

Toby Maloney

The Violet Hour, Chicago IL, USA

gaz sez: *Toby Maloney came to take my Cocktails in the Country bartender workshop in 2005, if memory serves. Philip Ward was in that class, too. Both of them have gone on to become superstar bar owners, but I doubt that my tutelage had anything to do with their successes. The opposite is, perhaps, the case here.*

Toby took the workshop again the following year, as did Phil Ward, and they were joined by a whole mess of top-notch bartenders: Lynette Marrero, Chad Soloman, Christy Pope, Marcos Tellos, Naren Young, Nicholas Jarrett, Sam Ross, and Tad Carducci, to name a few. I learned more about mixology that year than I had learned in all of my 30+ years behind the bar.

Hopefully these bartenders learned stuff from me about how to be of service and a few other things besides, but when it came to creating drinks, this group had it all over me.

Toby was the guy who approached me after the workshop and made a few suggestions on how to change the course a little in order to make it more valuable to 21st-century bartenders, and although I didn't follow all of his suggestions, I did listen, and the following year I changed the workshop completely.

Thank you, Toby. You're a Fabulous Bartender. Here's what Toby has to say for himself:

Q: How long have you worked behind the bar?

A: I poured my first drink in 1979 but didn't get behind a stick until 1992.

Q: Name the bars where you worked, and what cities they are in.

A: Blue Mesa, Chicago; Soul Kitchen, Chicago; The Sanctaury, Khoa Lanta, Thailand; Mas, Chicago; Grange Hall, NYC; Eugene, NYC; Flow, NYC; Dorsia, NYC; Milk & Honey, NYC; Freeman's, NYC; Flatiron Lounge, NYC; Pegu Club, NYC; Sb3, NYC; The Violet Hour, Chicago; Brad Street Craftshouse, Minneapolis; The Patterson House, Nashville; Bar Down Stairs, NYC; Hotel Williamsburg, Brooklyn.

Q: What do you love, and what do you hate, about bartending?

A: I love the social and the creative elements. I love making things that make people happy. I love the physicality and the feeling of being in the weeds. I hate what's it's done to my knees and elbows, and I hate counting money at the end of the night.

Q: What advice would you give to people who want to become bartenders?

A: Read, everything you can find, not just cocktail books. You are in the hospitality industry, you happen to serve drinks as well. Nobody likes a whiner. There is always more to learn.

Q: In what direction do you see the craft going in the next 5 years?

A: I'm not sure where it's going I just am so happy it's getting bigger.

Q: Anything else you'd like to add?

A: We are the luckiest people on earth to work in such a great industry. Appreciate it, be nice, and over-tip.

Chapter 5

Bar Blogs of the Year

I've picked some of my favorite blog postings of the year, for all sorts of different reasons, some because they've brought new facts to light, some because of the writer's commitment to good service, and some because of their groundbreaking ideas. All of them, however, are potentially very beneficial to our craft, and for that, on behalf of bartenders worldwide, I thank each and every contributor. All of the bloggers whose work appears below have given me their blessing to reprint their material, and you'll find links to their blogs at http://tinyurl.com/AM4Bartenders2012. I heartily encourage you to subscribe to these blogs—they stand out among the myriad bar bloggers out there.

Obviously, there will be many great bar blog postings that I've missed, and that will, unfortunately, always be the case. If you know of a blog, or better still, a specific blog posting, that you think I should consider for next year's *Annual Manual*, please send me a link: gaz@ardentspirits.com.

Here, then, are the four best bar blogs of the year—in my 'umble opinion, that is.

Alcademics.com

What is Fernet?
by Camper English, July 29, 2011.

By far the most famous type of fernet is Fernet-Branca, but there are other fernets on the market. So what is fernet, generally speaking?

(Thanks to commenter Scott who wrote in on the "Shhh It's a Secret" seminar at Tales of the Cocktail write-up for asking the question that I never thought to ask.)

I asked John Troia, co-founder of Tempus Fugit Spirits. They have a fernet coming out, Angelico Fernet. Here's what he says.

I'm sure there may be varying degrees of opinion, but we feel that the following is reasonably consistent with our research and that of others: Although categorized under Italian Amari (Bitters), Fernet is its own bitter category and is most often listed under Elixir/Elisir in Italian liquor manuals, when not simply called 'Fernet'. The extremely bitter (amarissimo is an apt description) concoction has its origins most often attributed to Bernadino Branca, who commercialized it in 1845, but conflicting data conjectures its creator(s)as : a mythical doctor/collaborator of Branca from Sweden named Fernet (possibly as an off-shoot of the older and better tasting 'Swedish Bitters'); Maria Scalia, the wife of Bernadino Branca who was a master herbalist and self-taught doctor; a monk named Frate Angelico Fernet who may have been responsible as the origin of many herbal tonics and elixirs (Fernet being a historical French Burgundy surname—pronounced Fair-Nay- and which underwent many spelling transformations); and a modern Italian liquorist text-book reference to it having originated somewhere in Hungary.

Fernet was most likely created to counteract the effects of Cholera and Malaria, but went on to be used for everything from a laxative to hangover cure. Today, as in the past, there are many Fernet producers (with the largest making so much of the world's production that some actually believe Fernet is a brand-name), but mostly made in tiny quantities for local rural Italian consumption. The various known recipes most typically share ingredients such as Aloe, Saffron, Quinquina, Gentian, Anise, Angelica, Mint and the odd Larch/White Agaric, a type of tree-bark loving mushroom (once also known as Spunk) rarely used or even found commercially outside of Italy. This latter ingredient (along with Saffron) seems to define and create the backbone of the best Fernets; Agarico mondo has an odd, bitter taste that becomes lightly mentholated on the mid-palate and was used to treat night-sweats.

According to Abruzzo's local doctor, pharmacist, winemaker, distiller and bitter-maker Marchese Dottore Egidio Niccolo Antonio d'Alesasndro di Trasmondi, the best Fernets have little or no sugar in them as it impairs digestion.

Thanks John—any questions?

> **gaz sez:** *Although Camper puts out tons of fabulous information on a very regular basis—he has my head spinning at times—this blog posting, for me, was one of the most groundbreaking stories of 2011. Fernet is a category? Who the hell knew that? Thanks, Camper, and John Troia, of course, for helping to bring this to our attention.*

Bar Life UK

Hey old timer - Shut up by The Gooch, January 12, 2011.

Allow me to start this rant with a thank you.

A thank you to all of the old guard for what they have done for our industry: From the early days of expanding the popularity of quality spirits and cocktails, for working tirelessly to educate and train up and coming bartenders, and for making the bartending profession a respected one.

With that said, I would like to say to a small but growing section of the old guard – Shut The F**k Up!

Over the past 12 months it seems that more and more of our industry's well respected and well loved characters have been busy spending their time telling us all how lucky we are and how good we have it. If I wanted to hear that I'd visit my Grandpa – quite frankly I expect better from people that have been there and done it.

You've told us all how lucky we are, now let me take this opportunity to put the record straight. Seeing as how most people who have been saying this haven't pulled a back-to-back double shift weekend behind a bar in the last 10 years, maybe they too will learn something about the life of a modern day bartender.

Yes we do have access to more training and knowledge than you ever had, and yes we are very grateful to be able to learn as much as we can so easily.

However firstly let's not forget that most of this training is being paid for by the World's drinks companies, and has given several of you folks a very nicely paid job in the twilight of your bartending careers.

Secondly, with training comes expectation and whilst it is true that a very good level of knowledge is now much easier to come by than in days of yore, it is also true that to stand out from the pack from a knowledge point of view is harder than ever before. How do we do this? By reading, by asking, by experimenting, by doing what you all did back in the day to stand out from your peers.

Yes the consumer is more knowledgeable than ever before. Yes you were instrumental in helping that happen.

You know what though folks, you created a fucking monster. Like a football supporter on the terraces knows how to manage the team better than the manager thanks to the non-stop flow of data coming their way, now our customers think they know more about cocktails than we do.

Just as a football fan doesn't know more about managing a team than Fabio Capello…. (okay bad example)… Alex Ferguson – Dave and Sandra probably don't know more about how an Aviation is made than a top bartender ('not like that, it's got Jager in it, I read it on the Internet!').

Yes we do have more products behind the bar than ever before giving us access to more cocktails and creations.

You know what though? More spirits means more cocktails being created which means a whole lot more recipes to remember – not just the classics of your day, but modern classic and the drinks you lot all invented plus our own concoctions.

It also means a whole lot more crap brands to get onto our lists because the owners have done a deal with certain brand owners. To top it off, all those brands on our back bar need a basic understanding by us lot in front of them, which means more of that much loved knowledge to store in our Playstation-addled brains.

Yes there are more opportunities for us, more competitions with better prizes and general goodies being thrown our way.

Thanks for that – I didn't say you were all bad!

It has also warmed the tiny cockles (I said cockles stop that giggling on the back row) of my heart to see that more than one of the old guard have stood up for us recently, seemingly noticing the nonsense some of their peers have been knobbing on about. Namely, thank you Gaz Regan with your Bar-Tweenies article for the San Francisco Chronicle and Naren Young in Australian Bartender Mag and www.4bars.com.au.

Both were spot on in their view that whilst we don't have it necessarily easier than those before us some in our industry do look at their bartending careers as if they were an inspiring pop act on X Factor.

It takes time and dedication to reach the dizzying heights that both of these guys have achieved and there is no such thing as a quick fix. True bartenders completely understand this and as we do not judge all our predecessors by the examples of certain money grabbing dicks, we would appreciate not all being judged by some fly by night young cock jockeys as Gaz and Naren have managed to do.

Finally, no we don't all wear waistcoats and greet every customer with a bow and a 'good evening sir and madam I take it your day was pleasant'.

But then again we don't use lime cordial and get to work on a horse – times change. We will greet our customers as the bar dictates – always politely, always graciously but not always like we have a plum inserted in our rectum.

gaz sez: *There's so much to comment on in this blog that I don't know where to begin. Thanks to Gooch, whoever he or she may be, for shouting me out as one of the good guys, but I should add that I've also been a bit guilty of saying, "you've no idea how lucky you are," too. Part of that comes from the fear of all this going away. I well remember the "aha!" moment I had at the London Bar Show in 2006 when I realized that the stuff that I, and many, many others in the business, had been pushing towards for years had actually come to pass. Bartenders were at last being recognized as craftspeople, and a huge number of bartenders were taking the job very seriously indeed. My immediate reaction was: "how do we make sure it stays that way?"*

I needn't have worried, as it turns out. Why? Because the twenty-first-century bartenders who made all this come true have also been responsible for making sure it's not going anywhere soon. I'm old enough to remember the rise of celebrity chefs back in the 1970s, before which time James Beard and Julia Child were just about the only nationally-known chefs in the USA (Fanny Craddock and Clement Freud, I guess, were their UK counterparts). Now, of course, we have dozens of chefs whose names are known by near-as-damn-it everyone in their native country, and the same thing is happening in the world of the celebrity bartender. It didn't go away for chefs, and it's not going to go away for bartenders, either.

It's worth noting here, I think, that apart from present-day bartenders' passion for their craft, there's one more thing that's keeping this movement alive: Money and support from liquor companies small and large. I, for one, will be the first to tell you that without the money I make from judging competitions and myriad other chores I do for liquor companies, I wouldn't be able to bring out this manual every year. I don't do any work for products I consider to be inferior, and at the same time I always remember who is helping me put bread on the table. If you are a bartender who gets corporate support in any way at all, I urge you to always remember who brought you to the dance.

Keep up the good work, guys. You've done wonders for our craft in the past decade or so. And don't forget: I'll still give any one of you a run for your money when the joint's six deep and the bar-back didn't show up . . .

Drinks.SeriousEats.com

From Behind the Bar: On Hospitality
by Michael J. Neff, July 27, 2011.

New Orleans is a beautiful city, and I was lucky enough to spend a few days there recently. I was traveling on business, but since I work in a bar, that business involved cocktails. For those of you who haven't heard of it, Tales of the Cocktail is an annual bacchanal/convention that brings together people from all over the world to learn about, sample, discuss, and generally celebrate spirits and how we use them.

The event is headquartered at the storied Hotel Monteleone, which is conveniently located around the corner from a much earthier establishment, Acme Oyster House. Their specialty (besides oysters, obviously) is a massively decadent po' boy sandwich called The Peace Maker. While my nights were occupied walking the streets drinking Abita Amber from a plastic cup, each day started sitting at the Acme Bar and fortifying myself with fried shrimp and oysters on a roll. Yes, I want tartar sauce. Of course, I'll take the coleslaw. Absolutely, I'd like to wash that down with a cold beer.

The French Quarter was overrun with cocktail-types for five days, to the delight and chagrin of actual working bartenders who operated the establishments we all would frequent. Delight, because bartenders are famous for being generous tippers, and can often be compassionate customers. Chagrin, because we can also be royal pains-in-the-ass if things aren't going the way we think they should. The last thing any bartender on the planet needs to do is instruct a New Orleans bartender in the making of a proper Sazerac, but I saw it happen. The consequences were amusing for me, but embarrassing for the poor sap who thought to open his mouth. C'est la vie.

Of the bartenders I met working in The Big Easy, the man behind the bar at the Acme was by far the most impressive. Big and burly, with waist-long dreadlocks, he poured beers (often), made cocktails (occasionally), served up food (constantly), and ran an incredibly tight ship while keeping his cool, and making sure everyone had exactly what they needed.

What sold me was how he presented the check. He would look his guest in the eye, shake their hand, and say, "Y'all come back and see us any time." On my second visit, he said, "I'll see you back here tomorrow, right?" And he was right. I went back every day, in no small part due to the experience I had watching him work his bar.

What most people call lunch, I call breakfast, and it's a meal I tend to prefer alone. As I enjoyed my day's fortification, I had plenty of time to reflect. At the exact same time our fancy New York cocktail bars were being nominated for awards celebrating how awesome we are, this man was working his own brand of magic, brilliantly demonstrating that many of us miss the point.

Think about the last time you were in a bar where you were not known, and the bartender reached out and shook your hand. How often will a mixologist look up from the execution of his "mixology" when someone new bellies up? The phrase most necessary, but least often heard, in cocktail bars is "How are you enjoying your drink?" If we changed the yard-stick on how bars are measured from cocktails to hospitality, many of the establishments that won awards that weekend would find themselves soundly drubbed by little dives in places like New Orleans, Wichita, and Phoenix.

This is unfortunate for cocktail makers and imbibers alike. I love making cocktails as much as I love drinking them, but their creation is not my primary job. The first purpose of every bar, cocktail or otherwise, is to provide an enjoyable experience for our guests. It starts and ends with hospitality. Period.

We forget that to our detriment. The cocktail has been elevated to culinary heights, which is a wonderful thing for all of us. The problem arises when they are elevated past the level of those who drink them. I am lucky to have trained many people who will go off in to the world to be fantastic bartenders. This process takes years sometimes, and the last thing I ever talk about is how to make cocktails. Compared to consistently delivering genuine hospitality to every single guest who walks in the door, day after day, making cocktails is a piece of cake.

My trip was illuminating. I tasted new spirits, compared notes with fellow travelers, and generally immersed myself in the collective culture of cocktails in this country. The best thing, though, was watching the bartender at The Acme. He reminded me that the bar for true hospitality is set very high, and I am grateful for the reminder. Hopefully, everyone else was paying attention as well.

> **gaz sez:** *Michael J Neff is an absolutely beautiful soul, and it was tough to pick from his blogs when I had to decide which one to reprint here. I really urge you to sign up for his missives at Drinks.SeriousEats.com so that you don't miss a word of what Michael writes.*
>
> *In the piece above, Michael gets to the very heart of our chosen craft when he highlights the Acme's bartender. Especially when you remember that he was attending Tales of the Cocktail, the big-*

gest event of its kind in the USA, he'd been surrounded by big-shot bartenders from all over the world, attending lectures and workshops hosted by the best of the best in our industry, and still he says, "The best thing, though, was watching the bartender at The Acme." If you want to be a bartender who people remember, it's a good idea to put a lot of energy into the hospitality side of our craft.

StarChefs.com

History, Hotels, and New (Old) Horizons: The Roots of Room Temperature Cocktails by Emily Bell with Will Blunt, November 2011[2]

Like most things sinful, strong, and drinks-related, hotel (or flask, or, most accurately, room temperature) cocktails have mired history. These boozy, iceless concoctions are often consumed by traveling bartenders, and have roots in everything from modern "go cup" Nola Street drinking to pre-ice cocktail culture (the Kold Draft and Scotsman-free dark ages before "Ice King" Frederic Tudor inaugurated commercialization of the cold stuff). Having taken more than a few room temperature sips for ourselves, we haven't found a single seed at the root of the resurgence of the iceless cocktail. Instead, and like most mixological phenomena, it seems to be the step-child of several cocktail themes, belonging entirely to none.

A Cocktail by Any Other Name

"Originally for me, they were flask cocktails," says Chris Hannah, tuxedoed barman at New Orleans' Arnaud's French 75, whose iceless "The Rebennack" tarts up rye whiskey and Averna with a dose of Creole Shrubb. "Next I hear they're called hotel cocktails—and this stems from what bartenders carry to hotels on our cocktail events." Hannah here refers to the practice (or inevitability) of bartenders gathering and mixing over the course of mixology happenings—none so grand as

---

2   Copyright © 1995-2011 StarChefs. All rights reserved.

Tales of the Cocktail. "We bring all of our checked liquor to a room and make do with what we [have]."

Sounds simple enough. But just over on Freret Street, beta cocktails coauthor and Cure barman Kirk Estopinal serves a drink called the "Hotel Room Temp" that's actually not an homage to the hotel mixing phenomenon. Instead, it pays respect to another cocktail, a motel cocktail, the "Days Inn Daiquiri," created by vacationing fellow mixo Kyle Davidson of The Violet Hour. Unlike your typical good-times daiquiri, Estopinal says his cocktail is "the finale drink in a hopelessly depressed outlook on love," adding "maybe there's a philosophy for room temperature cocktails in there—as if room temperature drinks are the desperate alcoholic affairs signaling the end of a party."

High Test History

Estopinal's guess might have a depressingly "desperate times" connotation, but according to at least one cocktail family tree, he's not far off. At a recent mixology conference, Hannah heard Alconomics guru Angus Winchester ("he gives the very best cocktail seminars in the industry, period") relate room temperature cocktail to the Scaffa, a historic cocktail category that's variously qualified as being a pousse-café type mixture of "brandy, maraschino, and/or another liqueur" (Dave Wondrich), or a boozy, layered cocktail crafted with a "'whatever's in the cupboard'" mentality (Winchester). In the latter definition, the Scaffa is the drinkable lovechild of thirst, empty cabinets, and ingenuity. And while it's nowhere defined as being strictly iceless (except for Jerry Thomas's "Brandy Scaffa," Wondrich notes), the resourceful creativity of the Scaffa does seem to square with the thrown-together magic of the room temperature cocktail.

And then, of course, there are scattered hints that the room temperature cocktail was something else, to someone else, sometime in the past. At Brooklyn's The Counting Room, Cure alum and fellow beta cocktails man Maks Pazuniak says he "had an elderly gentleman once ask me for something he called an 'Evening Cocktail.' I asked 'What does that mean? Do you want something neat?' He says 'No, a cocktail. No ice.' I assume he wanted it up. I started adding ice to my mixing glass and he stopped me. 'No ice at all.'" Pazuniak, who'd only tasted his first room temperature cocktail a couple years before, answered the request with the silk and structure of an ice-free "Charlatan" (and never heard the name 'evening cocktail' again).

Tasting Tepidity

But as any good mixologist—or dedicated drinker—knows, the success of a cocktail has much less to do with the name than what's in the glass, or, in the case of the room temperature cocktail, what's not in the glass. In an age where Thomas's cube, cracked, shaved, and block ice styles have evolved into a kind of hyper-particular ice purism, the total absence of ice, in both prep and service, makes for a strangely refreshing cocktail experience. Pazuniak got his first ice-free sip courtesy of 2011 Houston Rising Star Bobby Heugel, who served him his favorite (and Anvil's only cocktail mainstay) "The Brave". "It contradicts people's expectations of what a drink should be," says Heugel. "But we do it on purpose."

Heugel isn't just messing with his patrons. Room temperature cocktails have more aromatic volatility than the chilled alternative (for certifiable in-depth analysis, check out Taste Buds and Molecules by taste guru Francois Chartier). Just like wine, when a spirit or concoction is warmer, its volatile aromatic compounds escape more easily, meaning the Chichicapa Mezcal and Averna Amaro can show more of their herbaceous, fruit, and/or smoky notes in "The Brave" than they might in a cold cocktail. The trick for any mixologist going ice-free is playing around.

Playtime for Grown-Ups

And that might be what sparked renewed interest in the room temperature cocktail. "It's an experiment," says Estopinal, who says he first heard about iceless cocktails "in the hushed conversations of serious bartenders, about where it's all going." In theory, the room temperature context allows masters of the craft (with a penchant to play) to manipulate the sensory experience of a cocktail in new ways.

Among the options? Temperature. "Some people are shooting for 58 to 65°F, ambient room temperature, in order to make the drink better, more or less aromatic," says Estopinal. Another key factor in the aromatics: dilution. "Some people will tell you [room temperature cocktails] should be diluted, and others say they shouldn't," says Pazuniak. Not adding water makes for a more potent concoction, but as any Scotch drinker knows, water can also open up or soften the aromatics of a spirit—a rough equivalent to instant decanting (though technically speaking, water reacts with starch, its presence in a spirit or cocktail can alter the aromatic dynamic). In a recipe for one of his room temperature cocktails, Alchemy Consulting's Troy Sidle proposes a compromise: add "just enough water to remove the burn of the bourbon but not too much to needlessly dilute it." And with those two factors, obviously, comes the booze itself. Most of the room temperature cocktails we tasted have richer base spirits, simpler construction, and (so far) absolutely no citrus (though Pazuniak is currently mulling over some ideas).

Whatever it's called, and however it's served (we've had it in plastic cups, rocks glasses, and wine glasses), the end result of all this playing around is a rich, potent cocktail that seems more suited to educated sipping than cocktail happy hour—hence the industry-only culture. And if and when room temperature cocktails are served outside of bartender-and-booze-packed hotel rooms—"my guess is they'll get on menus," says Arnaud—the key is keeping patrons apprised not only of their unusual temperature, but their special potency. As for the name? Call them what you want. Just hold the ice.

The Brave Mixologist

Bobby Heugel, Anvil Bar & Refuge, 1424 Westheimer Road, Houston, TX 77006

Adapted by StarChefs.com, June 2011

Yield: 1 Cocktail

INGREDIENTS:

1 ounce Del Maguey chichicapa mezcal

1 ounce Hacienda del Sotol Plata tequila

0.5 ounces Averna amaro

1 barspoon Grand Marnier

3 mists Angostura bitters

1 flamed orange zest

METHOD: Combine the mezcal, tequila, Averna, and Grand Marnier in a wine glass without ice and swirl together. Mist three small amounts of Angostura Bitters on top. Garnish with the flamed orange zest.

The Charlatan

Mixologist Maksym Pazuniak, Maison Premiere, 298 Bedford Avenue, Brooklyn, NY 11211

Adapted by StarChefs.com, November 2011

Yield: 1 Cocktail

INGREDIENTS:

2 ounces Punt e Mes vermouth

3/4 ounce Campari

¾ ounce Cherry Heering

2 dashes Regan's orange bitters

3 swaths orange peel

METHOD: Mix the above ingredients in a mixing glass with no ice. Flame 3 swaths of orange peel inside a rocks glass, coating the inside of the glass with the oil. Pour the contents of the mixing glass into the rocks glass, and garnish with a single un-flamed orange twist.

The Rebennack

Mixologist Chris Hannah, Arnaud's French 75, 813 Bienville Street, New Orleans, LA 70112

Adapted by StarChefs.com, November 2011

Yield: 2 Cocktails, Enough for 1 Flask

INGREDIENTS:

4 ounces Rye Whiskey

1 ounce Averna

¾ ounce Creole Schrubb

METHOD:

Combine all ingredients, without ice, stir, and transfer to a flask using a funnel.

The Hotel Room Temperature

Mixologist Kirk Estopinal. Cure, 4905 Freret Street, New Orleans, LA 70115

Adapted by StarChefs.com

November 2011

Yield: 1 Cocktail

INGREDIENTS:

1 ½ ounces Carpano Antica vermouth

3/4 ounce El Dorado 12 Year rum

½ ounce Marie Brizard orange curaçao

14 drops Bittermens Xocolatl Mole Bitters

orange peel

METHOD: Combine the ingredients in a rocks glass. Stir and pour between two rocks glasses a few times. Serve in one of the glasses with a peel of orange skin that has been expressed on the glass, but not into the drink. Hang the peel on the glass artfully.

gaz sez: *This is a movement I really like. Bold, strong drinks are right up my alley, and I love the fact that bartenders this year are jumping onto this particular bandwagon and creating new room-temperature drinks. Hopefully these new potions might get more consumers interested in the category.*

I've been drinking a mixture of cognac and ruby port, at approximately a 50:50 ratio, since I was in my twenties—a very long time ago—and I've always thought of the drink as being a digestive. Indeed, I've employed it to quell queasy tummies on more than a few occasions, and although I'm reticent to recommend booze as a medicinal tonic, I've seen people recover from a tummy-ache almost instantaneously after quaffing one of these babies. Best of all, it tastes good, too.

The one aspect of room-temperature drinks to bear in mind if you're thinking of creating something along these lines is that it's a good idea to incorporate a goodly pour of low-alcohol ingredients since you don't have water from melted ice to help bring the alcohol percentage down when you make these. It's going to be interesting to see where this category of drinks goes in the next few years.

THE MORTIFYING INCIDENT

"Andrew Johnson, most unfortunately for himself, was intoxicated when sworn in as Vice-President of the United States . . . That he admitted his lapse at the outset is evident from the fact that he preserved the proof among his own manuscripts; and doubtless both he and his devoted wife mourned the mortifying incident and resolved that such conduct should not be repeated. ."

—*President Johnson and Posterity* by James Schouler. Found in *The Bookman: An Illustrated Magazine of Literature and Life*, 1912.

Part 3

Bar Geekery

A QUART BOTTLE OF GIN COCKTAIL

With the coming of June it was again time for me to cross the ocean once more. The day before I betook myself to the good ship Parthia, the maid handed me a package with 'Something for you, Miss!' It was a quart bottle of gin cocktail! Within an hour another bottle arrived, and later on yet another! They all bore the label of one Billy Pitcher— known to the male sex as a famous expert in cocktails. What did it mean? Why should I be the innocent recipient of all this compromising liquor?

—*Memories of a Musical Career* by Clara Kathleen Rogers, 1919.

Chapter 1

Scuppered: A Tale of the Bar Rail

In November, 2011, I received the following email from Peter Vestinos, owner of The Bar Medic, a consulting company in San Francisco:

> Hi Gary: I've been dealing with a language barrier of sorts during a project I have been consulting on in Chicago. The issue, has actually made me rethink a key piece of bar equipment and I was hoping to get your help. When designing the bar, we were looking at the bar top and the sides of the bar top (the side facing the guest and the side facing the bartender). The side facing the bartender, that bar lip, where we do our work, I referred to as the "bar lip" or "inside bar rail". The architects refer to it as a "scupper rail" which I had never heard before, and someone else calls it the "peanut rail" (which in itself brings up a bunch of curious possibilities...).

So, I thought maybe you could post something in your newsletter to see what people call this and to see if we do have a definitive name for this bar lip.

Thanks, Peter Vestinos

This looked geeky enough for me to explore the subject further, especially since I've always called that trough, well, I never really had a name for it to be honest. I've usually thought of it as the "well where I work" rather than the "well where I keep generic booze for the poor slobs who don't designate a decent brand."

Interested to hear what others had to say about the "scupper rail," I opened the subject up for discussion via my eLetter, and I was delighted to see a plethora of responses with many fun suggestions and notions.

Before we get into the notions sent to me by other folk, I should mention that I did a little research into the word scupper, and without going into the boring details that I uncovered, let me just say that a scupper was originally a nautical term used to describe drainage that allowed water to flow off the decks of ships into the sea. I can't find reference to it prior to the early 1800s. I do like the word, though.

A few people, including Dermot Walsh, my third cousin who isn't involved in the bar business at all, and Geraldine Coates, she who rules GinTime.com, a very fine web site, indeed, assured me that the word scuppered, where they hailed from (Lancashire and Scotland, respectfully), was used to describe a person who was, well, tired, worn out, completely shagged, that kind of thing.

Anthony DeSerio, an old friend, even though I never do seem to recognize the man when I bump into him, told me that he heard the following yarn from "an old carpenter" who used to frequent one of the bars where Anthony worked:

I was informed that back when bars and saloons were built they were directly made to the exact height of the owner of said joint. The Scupper Rail was actually on the outside of the bar top next to the customer as they were doing most of the spilling anyway. What was most interesting to me was that the height of the bar was as he told me gauged by the height of the bartender. so that when he placed a glass in the channel of the scupper rail, his line of sight (looking through said glass) he would see a line that would indicate the proper pour into the glass prior to shot glasses having marks on them. When the bartender would pass on or sell his business to another, the carpenter would have to come back to see how the new bartender "measured up" and would therefore have to "raise or lower the bar" to accommodate the new owners pour and save loss of profit and insure accuracy. And that's my tale of the scupper rail…

Thanks Anthony. You're almost as gullible as I….

A variety of people including Jen Baker, Beverage Program Manager for Princess Cruises; Marianne Cozzi, a woman I worked with at The Spotty Dog Bar and Unisphere Cocktail Lounge, New York; Natalia Cardenas, who reached out to her fabulous circle of friends; Andy Gould, a bar owner and consultant in Chicago; Christofer Moustakas, a Greek bartender who, at the time of this writing, is looking for a gig in Manhattan; Pete Valavanis, of Cary's Lounge in Chicago; Steven Dean Lauria, of Los Angeles; Chris Halleron from Hoboken—a guy who no longer works behind the stick but will be a bartender for the rest of his life whether he likes it or not— Joel Lee Kulp, Owner & General Manager of The Richardson, Brooklyn; Pete Slade of Fling International Bar Services in Stamford, England;

and Jeff B. Katz of the Katz [Restaurant Design] Company in Denver offered the following terms that might be used for the aforementioned trough:

drip rail

inside rail

eaves trough

drip trough

peanut rail

the spill

bar lip

drink (s) rail

speed rail

gutter

collection plate

bar trough

working rail

gaz sez: *Personally I'm quite taken by the name scupper rail, but I have to say that the following letter made me accept that peanut rail is more appropriate, simply because it seems to be internationally acceptable, and because we live in such a small world these days that that counts for a lot.*

Dear gaz,

I open about 6 or 7 bars around the world each year and have often been involved in the bar design. Internationally most builders, architects and, importantly, bartenders seem to recognize it being called a peanut rail.

This certainly helps with training in foreign climes where they can get confused about speed rails and other areas of the bar design. The peanut rail is the only place they should make the drink as it helps to catch any spillage and also as it's usually reinforced metal, it's the perfect place to bang your Boston shaker down without damaging often expensive bar counters.

As for the actual name, I remember asking many years ago about the very same thing and the most convincing reason given was that it is designed to catch up any excess bar debris that can then be cleaned at the end of a shift and acts as a dam between customers being clumsy with spillage and the nice clean ice well. Considering most bars used to serve peanuts to their patrons, it also acted to stop the pesky little salty buggers getting into the work station. Hence the name 'peanut' rail.

If there is some truth in it, I'd love to know.... as to calling it something else, I personally will continue to call it a peanut rail. It's how I've trained it for years and it seems to work well for me (and the trainees love my mime of a clumsy guest knocking nuts left, right and centre).

Hope this is of some help.

Cheers
Pete Slade
Senior Consultant
Fling International Bar Services, Stamford, England.

And the one and only Tobin Ellis, of Bar Magic in Las Vegas, backed up Pete's letter when he chimed in with: "I've always known it as the peanut rail. my foggy memory recalls something about a time when bars often had a barrel of peanuts for guests, that's where they threw shells (other than the floor.) In the 90s we always put/slid/pulled in tips there, not equipment/tins, etc." (Thanks to Natalia Cardenas for passing Tobin's comments along.)

So there you have it. It's the peanut rail. I still kinda like scupper rail, though . . .

Chapter 2

On Giggers & Jiggers & the Fine Art of Free-Pouring

It's time for me to get on my high-horse about jiggers again, and if you've been following anything I've said on the matter over past few years you'll know darned well that I'm not much of a fan of jiggering. Free-pouring, as far as I'm concerned, is a far more accurate way of measuring ingredients. Mind you, that was not the case when I entered the free-pouring round at 2011's finals of the G'Vine Gin Connoisseur program. I screwed up royally on that one. Let me tell you about it— there's a lesson to be learned from my disaster.

In 2010 I entered the same round, and with one exception—I deliberately over-poured one drink so I could tell the audience that the drink was for a heavy tipper—I did very well indeed. Ask Philip Duff. He was pretty impressed. Twelve months later, though, before I actually took the challenge, I spent some time looking at the recipes, and devising a written chart for myself so that, instead of looking at the recipes to see how many milliliters or ounces were called for, instead I'd see a list of numbers that told me what to "count to" in my head as I poured. So, a recipe that started out like this:

60 ml (2 oz) G'Vine Nouaison gin

30 ml (1 oz) dry vermouth

Should have ended up like this:

60 ml (2 oz) G'Vine Nouaison gin 4

30 ml (1 oz) dry vermouth 2

Since my "two-count" equals 30 ml or 1 oz.

I should never have done this. Why? Because I screwed up by thinking that my 4-count was 1 ounce rather than 2 ounces, so the recipe ended up looking like this:

60 ml (2 oz) G'Vine Nouaison gin 8

30 ml (1 oz) dry vermouth 4

I ended up pouring double the amount I should have poured for each and every drink. Philip Duff just shook his head and walked off into the night muttering. ...

The Lesson: Don't let yourself get intimidated by a competition. Act as though you're just behind your home bar on a busy night.

Before I start my rant about jiggering and why I hate it so, I'm bringing you the results of an experiment I conducted in December, 2011, after I treated myself to a decent assortment of jiggers to test.

Jiggery Pokery: The Ultimate Test

I decided to buy a range of jiggers in order to test them for accuracy, and I also purchased a Carolina Biological Supply Company Graduated Cylinder to do the measuring. Impressed? Me, too. How accurate is the Carolina Biological Supply Company Graduated Cylinder? I dunno. I used it for every jigger, though, and the company sure as heck has an imposing name, right?

Disclaimer

I conducted these tests in my kitchen over the course of a chilly December afternoon. Apart from the Carolina Biological Supply Company Graduated Cylinder, I didn't use any other technical equipment. When I poured to the 1-ounce mark on a jigger, I used my eyes to tell me when to stop. Chances are I poured a little under in some cases, and a little over in others. HOWEVER, and this a pretty big HOWEVER, I guarantee you that my pours were way more accurate than those of any bartenders working the service end at eleven in the P.M. on a Friday night. And I think they were probably more accurate than the vast majority of jiggered-pours at any bar at any time of the day or night. I had no customers breathing down my neck, I had a specific mission in mind, and I had the luxury of being able to take my time, repeating each experiment if I thought the result seemed skewed.

Methodology

I took a 16-ounce kitchen measuring cup, which I filled to the 4-ounce mark for each measurement.

I put a largish funnel into the top of the Carolina Biological Supply Company Graduated Cylinder so that I couldn't spill.

I poured from the measuring cup into each jigger to the desired mark.

Then, in order to make sure there was no spillage, I emptied the measuring cup and poured from the jigger back into the measuring cup, and from the measuring cup into the funnel on top of the Carolina Biological Supply Company Graduated Cylinder.

I took these steps so as to make sure there was no spillage, though in the case of the Kikkerland Aluminum Cube Jigger (see below), I admit to a little spillage when I was trying to get the darned thing to the measuring cup. It's a bastard to handle, is the Kikkerland Aluminum Cube Jigger.

For the purposes of this experiment, although one fluid ounce is equal to 29.574 milliliters, we're using 1 oz = 30 ml as our standard. Live with it.

Read on the see how each of the jiggers I tested performed.

Anchor Hocking Measuring Glass: I really wanted this one to be accurate. If I'm measuring ingredients when testing recipes, or when creating recipes, this is the kind of "jigger" that I like. There's no need to fill it to the top with a convex meniscus that makes it damned near impossible to get the thing to the mixing glass. No, you just fill it to the appropriate line on the side of the glass. And the lines are printed in red so that even these old eyes can't miss them. And that's not all, folks. There are four sets of lines on this baby so you can measure in ounces, milliliters, tablespoons, or teaspoons (and the teaspoon line offers ¼-cup and ½-cup measurements, too). The 1-ounce line gave me 32 ml, the 1 ½-ounce line yielded 46 ml, and the 2-ounce line gave me 60 ml on the nose. This is my new measuring device for testing and creating.

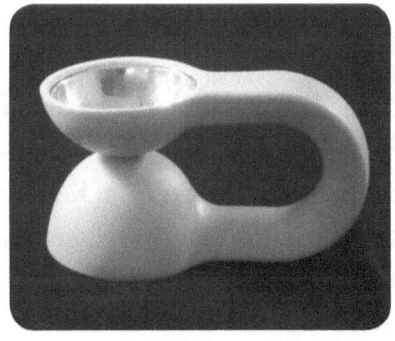

Ärta Dual-Ended Jigger: I wasn't expecting much from this one. Reminded me of a beautifully-etched bottle that's probably full of crap vodka, but hey, you never know till you actually taste the vodka, right? This one measures 1 ounce and 1 ½ ounces. The 1 ½-ounce end gave me 42 ml, and the 1-ounce end gave me 28 ml, so it was a little short in the sleeves, but not enough to send the whole suit back.

European Style Double Cocktail Jigger, 1 oz & 2 oz: I sorta like the looks of this one. It's all slick and slim and European-like. Got it from Kegworks, I did. There's no markings on it, but it's fairly obvious which end is 1 ounce and which holds 2 ounces, right? For ½-ounce measurements, or any measurements other than 1 or 2 ounces, you have to guess, but hey, that's what jiggering's all about, right? The 2-ounce side gave me 62 ml. Not bad, right? The 1-ounce side was spot-on. 30 ml on the dot. Not bad at all.

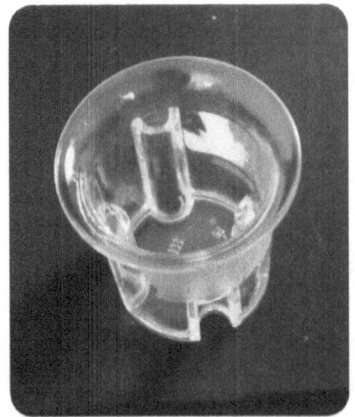

E-Z Step Cocktail Jigger: I really really really like the look of this one. The indentations make it really easy to pour with accuracy, providing the calibrations are correct, right? Here's how that went: The 1-ounce mark gave me 32 ml; 1 ½-ounce mark yielded 47 ml, and at the 2-ounce mark you get 63 ml. Not bad, I guess. Not bad.

Kikkerland Aluminum Cube Jigger: As with the ärta Dual-Ended Jigger, I wasn't expecting much from this cube jigger. Novelty item, I thought. The six sides of the cube offer the following measurements: ½-ounce, ¾-ounce, 1-ounce, 1 ½-ounces, 2-ounces, and 2 ¼-ounces. It was very hard to handle. The 2-ounce dent gave me 62 ml, which isn't too bad, I guess. The 1 ½-ounce dent rendered 49 ml (+ 4 ml). Not good. And the 1-ounce dent has enough room for 35 ml of hooch. Forget this one. It's now a paperweight on my desk.

The Original Multi-Purpose Mini Measure: Yes, it's a little shot glass. So shoot me already. The little darlin' measures in ounces, milliliters, teaspoons and tablespoons, and you don't have to fill it to the top to get 1 ounce, so there's no risk of spillage twixt pour and mixing glass. Filled to the 1-ounce mark this one gives you 27 ml.

Oxo Good Grips Mini-Angled Measuring Cup: I love the Oxo company. They issue innovative products that are simple to use, and they look good, too. The 1-ounce mark on this one gave me exactly 30 ml. Spot on. The 2-ounce mark yielded 62 ml. Not shabby, huh?

Oxo Steel Double Jigger: This jigger offers 1 ½-ounce, 1-ounce, ¾-ounce, ½-ounce, ⅓-ounce, and ¼-ounce options. It looks cool and nifty, and it's made by Oxo. Gotta be good, huh? 1 ½-ounce side gave me 46 ml which, as far as I'm concerned, is quite close enough. The 1-ounce side gave me just over 28 ml.

Trudeau 3-in-1 Measuring Jigger: I kinda like the look of this baby. Filled to the top it measures 2 ounces, and there are two ridges below so that it's possible to measure ½ ounce and 1 ounce. I tested just the 1-ounce and 2-ounce ridges and found them both to be just a tad inaccurate. The 1-ounce mark yielded 34 ml and the 2-ounce mark gave me 63 ml.

Uber Bar Tools Projig US Multi Measure Jigger: I know the guy who makes these. Michael Silvers. Nice chap. The first thing I didn't like about this one was that the measurements offered didn't translate too well unless you are willing to measure twice for most pours. The jigger offers compartments for the following measurements: ¼-ounce, ½-ounce, ¾-ounce, and 1 ¼-ounces. So, if you want 1 ounce you'll fill the ¼-ounce and ¾-ounce compartments, right? And since they are both on the same end of the jigger you can do this in one fell swoop—providing you can read the damned markings, that is. Oh, I know, if you work with it for an hour you'll soon know which compartment yields what, but a little black paint wouldn't go amiss on this baby. Filling the ¼- ounce and the ¾-ounce compartments should have given me 30 ml, right? Well that's exactly what I got. 30 ml on the nose. Next, I filled the 1 ¼-ounce, ¼-ounce, and ½-ounce compartments, yielding yet again precision accuracy of 60-ml. Thank God for that. I didn't want Michael to get pissed off with me…

The Very Nice Indian Jigger: There are no markings on this one, and it came with no instructions whatsoever so I've no idea how much each end is supposed to hold, but that doesn't really matter. This was a present from my good friend Tim Etherington Judge, the lad who helped me out at the 2011 Diageo World-Class finals in 2011. Thanks, Tim. This is my absolute favorite jigger.

Conclusions

Although, as you can see above, there were just two jiggers that I really hated, I have to say that the calibrations on these things were pretty darned good. Add in a small plus/minus factor and you could say that they all near-as-damn-it made the grade.

Reasons to Throw Away Your Jiggers

I have yet to see a bartender use a jigger properly. Not one. Ever. Every single bartender who I have witnessed using a jigger one makes a huge noise about demanding that the ingredients in this drink or that cocktail be measured with precise accuracy, and then they don't bother to fill the jigger to the top, or they fill it to the top then add another few drops. How accurate is that?

"I just use the jigger as a guideline," I'm frequently told.

And if that's the case, then you should know this: Free-pouring is just as accurate, if not more accurate, than jiggering if you don't use the jigger properly.

If you're going to use a jigger I have no objection, providing you use it in the way it was designed to be used. If you use it just as a "guideline," then I suggest that you get off your lazy ass and learn how to free-pour.

And before you start to moan about pour-spouts being different from each other, pouring at different rates which screws up your free-pouring "count," let me add this: Does every bar you've ever tended use the same size of cocktail glass? I presume that your answer is "no." and what do you do when faced with this? You adjust until you get it right. That's what you do.

gaz is proved wrong: Seconds before the Trusty Ms. M (Martha Schueneman, my trusty editor) got her hands on this chapter, I happened to see a video of Eben Freeman, the famed New York bartender who introduced fat-washing to us all not too long ago, making a Sidecar. He used his jiggers absolutely beautifully. Well done, Eben. You are the only guy I've seen do this thus far.

gaz totally missed this one: After emailing Eben to congratulate him on his jiggering technique, the bastard wrote back to bring up one more point about how to use these diabolical instruments properly, and damn it, he was right so I had to add this, too. All of this is going down while the Trusty Martha is in the middle of editing this tome, so now I have to bother her with yet one more addition to the manuscript. Sure as hell hope she doesn't get all school-marm'ly on me. Here's what Eben wrote:

"One more jigger abuse problem which is growing, bartenders do not rinse their jiggers between drinks. I sat at [FAMOUS Manhattan bar name deleted] one night and watched as they simply banged the jigger down between measures believing that would knock out any residual spirits, syrups and so forth—lazy. Do you want orgeat in your Manhattan?"

How to Learn to Free-Pour

Warning: This might take you the better part of twenty minutes. Maybe even half an hour. ...

In order to learn how to free-pour, take a bottle of water fitted with the same kind of pour-spout that you currently use at work. Pour water from the bottle into a measuring device with a 2-ounce calibration, and pour water into the receptacle until the water level reaches the 2-ounce mark.

Do that a couple of times, then start counting silently to yourself as you pour. Repeat this exercise over and over again until you have perfected a constant number that you reach every time the water hits the 2-ounce mark.

If you're really lucky, your number will be four, and if that's the case you'll know that you can count to "one" for half-ounce pours, etc.

When you are confident of your free-pour, test yourself by pouring into an empty glass with no calibrations, and then measuring the amount of water you've poured. Do this for all sorts of amounts until you're sure that you've got it.

And if you're wondering what to do with your jigger collection: Boil an egg for 3 ½ to 4 minutes and use your jigger as an egg-cup (as I do with the Indian jigger that some Limey bastard named Tim gave to me last year).

Ingredient Focus: Japanese Whisky

Note: Remember that you'll find lotsa links to sites relevant to this chapter if you go to http://tinyurl.com/AM4Bartenders2012.

I went to Japan in January, 2011, on a trip that was sponsored by the good folk at Suntory. Neyah White and Gardner Dunn, both ex-bartenders in the not-too-distant past who now work as ambassadors for Suntory, came on the trip, too, along with Yoshi Morita, Suntory's man in New York, and bar owner extraordinaire Greg Seider, a guy who sells lotsa Suntory whisky at the Summit Bar, his joint on Avenue C (near 8th Street) in Manhattan. What a blast we had.

Greg and I had a fabulous tourist day out in Kyoto. Mickey Fukui, our intrepid guide, showed us the delights of Kinkakuji (the Golden Pavilion), a Zen temple with two floors that are completely covered in gold leaf, and the Kiyomizudera Temple, a fabulous structure built in 780 that was originally associated with the Hosso sect, one of the oldest schools within Japanese Buddhism. We met a couple of very cool Japanese chicks there, too.

And, of course, we visited a few bars along the way. The High Five in Tokyo was, as expected, an incredibly great joint, and I even got to go behind the bar there with my brother, Hidetsugu Ueno, or Ueno-San, as he's known to most of us.

Last but not least was the Genroku bar in Kyoto, where I instantly fell head-over-heels for bartender Reiko Nakagawa. And you would have done the same thing, too. Promise.

I'm about to turn you over to Neyah White and Gardner Dunn, who will explain why Japanese whisky is different from all others, but just in case you happen to be new to the business, or perhaps you haven't gotten around to learning about the fine art of the distiller yet, I'm going to set down a very very basic primer on whisk(e)y production here. Ready?

Whisky starts its life, in a very real sense, as beer. Grains are always the base, and these are used to make a grain "soup," which is then fermented by the addition of yeast. This fermentation stage can also be referred to as mashing.

The yeast eats the starch in the grain and converts it to heat, alcohol, and carbon dioxide.

Before the mashing begins the grains are often malted to make it easy on the yeast. Malting involves treating the grain to a bath of water where it begins to germinate (a sprout grows from the individual grains). At this stage the starch is easier for the yeast to "digest."

To halt germination, the grain is heated. This can be done in a variety of ways, one of which is to heat the grains over a peat fire—a practice most common in the production of many scotch whiskies. Peat, basically rotted vegetation that's half-way to becoming coal, has a very smoky odor when it burns, and that odor can be transferred to the grain and make its way into the whisky.

The amount of smokiness (phenol levels) can be controlled by altering the length of time that the grain spends over the peat fire.

Grains heated by hot air will show no smoky characteristics.

After being malted, then, the grains are ready to be added to vats of water, and the yeast is then also added so that fermentation, or mashing, can commence.

Once the beer has fermented, it is distilled. Distillation is a very complicated affair, but the basic principle is this: alcohol boils (turns into vapor) at a lower temperature than water, so if you heat the beer to a temperature that's somewhere between the boiling point of alcohol and the boiling point of water, then the vapors that rise from the beer, when condensed back into a liquid form, will have a higher percentage of alcohol that the beer that you started with. Make sense?

The initial beer might have about 10 percent alcohol, and the resultant whisky, after a couple or three distillations in pot stills, could have about 70 percent alcohol.

Different shapes and styles of stills produce different styles of whisky, and we don't really have room to tell you much more than that here. Just take it from me, please. Such is the case.

Once distilled, and prior to any sort of marrying or blending, whisky is aged in oak barrels, and the species of oak used can make a tremendous difference to the finished product.

Single malt whisky is the product of just one distillery using 100-percent malted barley to make their whisky. This can be married to other single malts to make a pure malt, such as Johnnie Walker Green Label., and it can also be married to neutral grain whisky (more or less vodka but with a bit more flavor), to make a blended whisky (think Johnnie Walker Gold Label—my favorite blend). In the case of Japanese distilleries, as you're about to discover, many different single malts can be made at each facility.

I'll go deeper into distillation in a future issue of the *Annual Manual*, but for the time being I think you now have enough knowledge under your belt to understand the nuances that Neyah and Gardner are about to bring to you.

Overview of Japanese Whisky

by Neyah White and Gardner Dunn

It may seem like a silly thing to say, but the most important thing to remember when trying to understand Japanese whisky is that it is made for the Japanese people. The Japanese prefer to eat when they drink and being in Japan, they tend to eat Japanese food. This means that their whisky needs to be friendly to the varied subtle flavors common in the cuisine. As well, it means that the whisky needs to be crafted well enough to take on water, often bringing it down to the strength of beer or wine, and still show in the glass.

While we at Suntory certainly celebrate and are very proud of our single malts, Japanese whisky as a whole is based on blending. The Japanese consumer has no patience for tastes out of balance in general, and since the vast majority of the whisky consumed goes down stretched with water in the form of the Highball, the blenders are critical.

This obsessive attention to blending naturally shows up in the single malts as well in the fact that both of our distilleries make a huge variety of whisky types so that they have the tools to make balanced bottlings consistently. These different types are the result of decisions being made at every step of the process.

The first and most important decisions were made in 1923 and 1974, when selecting the sites to build the distilleries. The sites of both the Yamazaki distillery, and the Hakushu distillery, have tremendously pure, yet very different, water sources, and both provide for a unique and distinct character in the spirit. These waters impart their unique characters both during

At the fermentation, or mashing, stage there are two decisions to be made. We use two different yeast strains and both wooden and steel fermenting tanks. The differing yeasts provide different flavors in the initial distiller's beer, as do the different growing environments of wood and steel.

The next set of decisions gets even more involved. At Yamazaki and Hakushu we have six very distinct shapes of stills, and some use direct fire for heat while others use indirect heat. In turn, these stills are connected to two different styles of condensers. As a result, the range of spirits possible expands greatly as the various fermentation styles are run though the different still shapes.

Finally, as the new spirit goes to barrel, another very big decision needs to get made: what size and what type of barrel to use for aging. Smaller barrels give the whisky a bigger percentage of contact with the oak than large barrels, hence yielding different styles of whisky. We use five different barrel sizes made of wood from three different continents.

American Oak comes in the form of ex-bourbon barrels and new oak fashioned into large barrels known as puncheons. Made from white oak, these barrels are the most efficient aging vessels in play as the wood grain in the barrel staves is very tightly knit. American oak is known for the vanilla and caramel notes that it imparts into a spirit as it ages.

Spanish Oak comes in the form of butts that held Oloroso sherry. It is important to note that these are trees actually grown in Spain and a unique variety of oak, not American or Eastern European oak that has been seasoned with sherry. These grant us flavors in the style of the original whisky makers in the seventeenth and eighteenth centuries, who would use shipping barrels that had held fortified wines imported into the British Isles because the wood was cheap. Ours are hardly inexpensive, though. We work with a preserve in Spain and purchase trees before they are harvested, season the lumber for years, pay to have it coopered into barrels before it holds Oloroso sherry for a few years. Then the barrels are emptied and moved to Japan for whisky. Even though they have been seasoned with wine, these Spanish oak barrels are heavy with dark tannins and give us masculine flavors like dried fruits and tobacco.

The most unique wood source is Japanese Oak. We use barrels made from Mizunara, a species of water oak native to Japan that differs from white oak in shape and flavor influence. Spirit in these barrels is very slow to mature and these barrels are associated with a higher rate of evaporation than white oak barrels. This compounds the amount of whisky lost to the angels and makes it a very inefficient barrel to use. However, the incense and sandalwood aromas that this wood imparts just cannot be found anywhere else.

So, between the peating levels in the malt, the yeast strain, the fermenting vessel, the still shape, firing method, condenser style, barrel size, wood source and age, we make over 100 different whiskies in our distilleries. While our bottles may say "single malt" because we use 100-percent malted barley and pot stills in single facilities, there are many whiskies involved in their creation.

Why all this effort, the extreme range in wood influences, the wide variety of spirit styles? Because this is Japanese whisky for the Japanese people and it must fit into the Japanese lifestyle and sensibility. The careful and deliberate layering of flavors through all the various spirits produced is how this is achieved and why the blenders are so critical to Japanese whisky.

ABSTRUSE MATTERS OF SCIENCE & PHILOSOPHY

It was in my head somehow that Harry Hill's was where the savants were in the habit of meeting to commune upon abstruse matters of science and philosophy....

'Philosophers?' said they; 'why, there was never a philosopher there in the world! That is Harry Hill's, one of the worst dens in all New York. Those men were a very hard lot, except those country bumpkins that were skirmishing around there—flies in the web, and didn't know it—and the young girls were street-walkers, and the most abandoned in the city.'

When I found that I, a newspaper man, had been drawn into such a place as that, my indignation knew no bounds, and I said we would go and hunt up another one.

—Mark Twain, San Francisco,
Alta California, 1867.

INDEX OF BARTENDERS, BARS, & SUCH

A

A21 111
Alcademics.com 221
Anchor Hocking Measuring Glass 252
Apothecary 106
Aqua Vitae 179
Ärta Dual-Ended Jigger 253
Artesian Bar at The Langham Hotel 146

B

Bar Life UK 223
Bar Magic 207, 247
Bar Solution 164, 166
Beke, Marian 174
Bell, Emily 232
Berg, Monica 179
Bistro de l'Arte 73
Bistro Lancaster
 at the Lancaster Hotel 91
Blunt, Will 232
Bombay Club 150
Bovey, Daniel 103
Bristol Seafood Grill 84

C

Canon 183
Charming, Cheryl 150, 152
Church, Mark 89
Coco at the Roxy 97
Conejito's Place 81
Connaught Hotel 136

D

Daniel, Sarah 80

Death & Co 169, 171
Dehlavi, Cris 159
Del Diego 119, 120
Del Diego, Fernando 119, 120
Dino 91, 92
Drinks.SeriousEats.com 228, 230
Dunn, Gardner 263, 265, 267

E

Ellis, Tobin 207, 210, 247
Elmegirab, Adam 127, 129
Employees Only 163, 164
English, Camper 221
EO Brands 164, 165
Esmon, Phoebe 193
European Style Double Cocktail Jigger, 1 oz & 2 oz 254
E-Z Step Cocktail Jigger 254

F

Fausz, John 87
Fetcu, Mihai 73
Flip-It! Cocktail Mixologists 69, 70
Fulton, Fritz 90

G

Gardel's Bar 115
Griffiths, Merlin 75
Guirra, Lala 81

H

Halleron, Christopher "Hal" 155, 156
Huelsing, Ryan 84
HUM Spirits 133

I

Ivy, Level 6 109

J

Jack's Lounge 86
Judge, Tim Etherington 98, 259

K

Kammerling, Alex 140
Kamm & Sons 140
Kikkerland Aluminum Cube Jigger 252, 255
Kratena, Alex 146

M

Macao Trading Co 164, 165
Maloney, Toby 214
Martin, Paul "The Mixxa" 189
McDermott, Steve 203, 205
McGoram, Simon 115
Melton, Brian 82
M Restaurant 159, 160

N

Neff, Michael J. 228
Newman, Dave 113, 114
Nightjar 174, 177
Nobu 113

O

Onishi, Daisuki 106
Oxo Good Grips Mini-Angled Measuring Cup 256
Oxo Steel Double Jigger 257

P

Perrine, Joy 86
Perrone, Ago 136, 185
Petraske, Sasha 198
Philips, Tim D 109
Porteno 115
Priory Tavern 75

R

Reinstadtler, Eric 82
Restrepo, George 101

S

Sahara Bar 103
Sarva Yoga Academy 164
Seger, Adam 133, 135

Siitonen, Timo 111
Simo, Joaquin 169, 171
Simpson, Ben 97
Smith, Devin 88
StarChefs.com 232, 236, 237
Stenson, Murray 183, 185, 186
Stringer, Michael 69, 70
Suntory 119, 263, 268

T

Tag Restaurant 82
Tate's Craft Cocktails 82
The 86 Spirits Co 164
The Bowery 203, 205
The Davenport 80
The Farmer's Cabinet 193, 195
The Gooch 223
The Original Multi-Purpose Mini Measure 256
The Royale 87
The Union Cabaret & Grille 88
The Very Nice Indian Jigger 259
The Violet Hour 214, 216, 233
Trudeau 3-in-1 Measuring Jigger 257
Twilight 106

U

Uber Bar Tools Projig US Multi Measure Jigger 258

W

White, Neyah 119, 120, 263, 265, 267
Woodlands Tavern 90
Wunder Bar at Grunauer 89

Z

Zaric, Dushan 63, 163

BACKMATTERS

www.ingramcontent.com/pod-product-compliance
Lightning Source LLC
Chambersburg PA
CBHW020326170426
43200CB00006B/292